# Assessing Writing Skill

*Research Monograph No. 11*

Hunter M. Breland
Roberta Camp
Robert J. Jones
Margaret M. Morris
Donald A. Rock

*College Entrance Examination Board, New York, 1987*

Inquiries regarding this publication should
be addressed to Editorial Office, The College Board,
45 Columbus Avenue,
New York, New York 10023-6917.

Copies of this publication may be ordered from
College Board Publications, Box 886,
New York, New York 10101. The price is $14.95.

Cover photograph by Glenn Foss.

Library of Congress Catalog Card Number: 86-073022

ISBN: 0-87447-280-6

Printed in the United States of America.

# Contents

## Tables

## Project Working Committee

Brandeis University . . . . . | James Merod
| Bruce McKenna

Rutgers University at Camden . . Timothy Martin

Spelman College        Jacqueline Jones Royster

Texas A&M University . . . . Gwendolyn Gong

University of California
at Los Angeles . . . . . . . George Gadda

University of Vermont . . . . Tony Magistrale

# Preface

In 1966 the College Board published a timely monograph titled *The Measurement of Writing Ability*, written by Fred I. Godshalk, Frances Swineford, and William E. Coffman. The monograph was significant because the research investigation on which it was based was one of the few studies in the history of the assessment of writing skill in which a comprehensive set of writing samples was collected from the same students. The present investigation began with the idea of replicating the Godshalk study, as it has come to be called, since it was believed that major changes had occurred over 20 years in the way English composition is taught and in the way skills in it are assessed.

This report represents an attempt to determine the most effective methods for assessing the kind of writing skills needed in college courses in English composition. The skills involved are primarily those required for narrative, expository, and persuasive writing, though students at times are called upon to do other kinds of writing. We would not expect that the skills required for college freshman-year writing would be greatly different from those required for good performance in the last years of secondary school.

The list of authors on the title page of this report is one hint of the magnitude of the task involved in its preparation. But these authors represent only a portion of the effort. There were also 7 working committee members (who did indeed work), 12 additional instructors in the participating institutions who collected writing samples from students, 267 students each of whom wrote six essays for the project, 18 college English instructors who served as readers, several consultants, and numerous reviewers of the report. The project could not have been accomplished without the contributions of these many participants.

We started the project by talking to others with experience in the field of writing assessment, though we have not always accepted their recommendations: E. D. Hirsch, Jr., of the University of Virginia, William E. Coffman of the University of Iowa, and Stephen P. Witte and John A. Daly of the University of Texas at Austin provided especially helpful advice. Early on it became clear that there were more questions about how to assess writing skill than we could possibly answer in a single project. As the project developed, constant vigilance was essential to control the complexity so that the project would not sink of its own weight. We thank these persons for discussing the project with us, but they cannot be blamed for any shortcomings it may have.

The Project Working Committee of English professors and instructors from six postsecondary institutions suggested essay topics, gave advice, and provided the essential link to the students who supplied the data. Catharine Lucas of San Francisco State University and Stephen P. Witte of the University of Texas at Austin gave valuable advice on defining the writing domains and on the specific writing tasks used in the investigation. We knew that we would need several samples of each student's writing before we could accurately judge his or her level of writing skill. It was believed that the best way to obtain such a collection of writing samples would be in the classroom setting. The members of the working committee organized the data collections within their own institutions.

Special appreciation goes to the following instructors in addition to those who served on the working committee: Desmond McCarthy, Cynthia Lowenthal, and Jim Keil (Brandeis University); Karen Schramm and Paul Lisicky (Rutgers University at Camden); June Aldridge and Christine Sizemore (Spelman College); Larry Beason and Cindy Schnebly (Texas A&M University); and Robert Cullen, Faye Peitzman, and Diane Armstrong (UCLA).

We thank those who read and scored the writing samples: Kathleen Adamczk, Trenton State College; Donald Billiar, Union County College; Norman Bosley, Middlesex County College; Jim Brazell, Trenton State College; Nancy Bruno, Middlesex County College; Santi Buscemi, Middlesex County College; John Collins, Glassboro State College; Marilyn Collins, Glassboro State College; Michael Conlon, New York Institute of Technology; Carter Daniel, Rutgers University; Lalaji Deshbandhu, Gloucester County College; Susan McNamara, William Paterson College; RoseAnn Morgan, Middlesex County College; Timothy Morris, Rutgers University; Jerry Olsen, Middlesex County College; Ted Otten, Mercer County Community College; Mary Ann Palladino, Mercer County Community College; Donna Perry, William Paterson College; Ziva Piltch, Pace University; William Seaton, Thomas A. Edison State College; Jonathon Thomas, Trenton State College; William Walling, Rutgers University.

Special recognition needs to be given to Educational Testing Service colleagues who assisted with the project. Warren Willingham suggested some of the key data collections and analyses. Paul Rosenbaum helped design the data collection and conducted the analyses of variance from which reliability estimates were made. Linda Cook equated the English Composition Achievement Test special administration scores and adjusted other of the test's scores to remove essay components. Gertrude Conlan assisted in the development of the writing tasks. The readings were expertly organized and managed by Phyllis Murphy and her essay reading staff. Brent Bridgeman and John Mazzeo reviewed an early draft and made several useful suggestions. Linda Johnson superbly handled financial and other administrative matters throughout the project. Patricia Coleman prepared the manuscript with exceptional speed and accuracy with the assistance of Nancy Wolff.

Finally, we want to thank the students who participated in the study. While their work was part of their freshman English courses, a research investigation can at times introduce burdens that would not have been there otherwise. As far as we can tell, the students were motivated to write well, and some demonstrated extraordinary skill in writing. One student received 101 out of a possible 108 holistic score points from the nine English professors who read the six essays she wrote for the project.

On behalf of my coauthors, I express appreciation for the many contributions that were made.

Hunter M. Breland
Project Director

# 1. Introduction

Over the years writing skill has been appraised through two approaches: direct assessement and indirect assessment. Direct assessments are those in which a sample of an examinee's writing is obtained under controlled conditions and then evaluated by one or more judges, usually English teachers trained in making judgments about writing skill. Indirect assessments are so termed because an estimate of probable skill in writing is made through observations of specific kinds of knowledge about writing, such as grammar and sentence structure, although more advanced skills can also be observed. These indirect assessments are commonly made by means of multiple-choice questions. Thus, direct assessments tend to be associated with writing samples and indirect assessments with multiple-choice questions.

Diederich (1974) probably captured better than anyone else the reasoning behind the widespread use of writing samples for the assessment of writing skill:

*As a test of writing ability, no test is as convincing to teachers of English, to teachers in other departments, to prospective employers, and to the* public as actual samples of each student's writing, especially if the writing is done under test conditions in which one can be sure that each sample is the student's own unaided work. People who uphold the view that essays are the only valid test of writing ability are fond of using the analogy that, whenever we want to find out whether young people can swim, we have them jump into a pool and swim. (p. 1)

From this perspective, if one wants to know if any given individual can perform any given task, a test of performance in that task is what is needed. Coffman (1971) presented the same kind of argument for the academic context:

*The only way to assess the extent to which a student has mastered a field is to present him with questions or problems in the field and see how he performs. The scholar performs by speaking or writing. The essay examination constitutes a sample of scholarly performance; hence, it provides a direct measure of educational achievement. (p. 273)*

The logic of these kinds of arguments is so cogent that despite more than a half century of criticism by educational measurement specialists, the essay remains a principal means of evaluation in courses of instruction of all types. In recent years, in fact, the essay has gained more and more advocates as evidence of a decline in writing skills among high school and college students accrues with each day. Faced with this, we

---

Parts of this introduction are adapted from a previous report (Breland 1983).

find it difficult to deny that students need more exposure to writing, whether in the form of instruction or examination.

Also related to direct assessment are issues of national impact—the message that is implicitly sent to students and teachers by direct assessment used on a wide scale: If large numbers of students are required to produce compositions for assessments important for graduation, certification, or admission to higher levels of education, students will be encouraged to learn composition skills and teachers to teach them.

Nonetheless, the history of direct writing skill assessment is bleak. As far back as 1880 it was recognized that the essay examination was beset with the curse of unreliability (see Huddleston 1954; Follman and Anderson 1967). One of the first demonstrations of the reliability problem occurred in the 1920s when it was shown that the score a student received on a College Board examination could depend more on which reader read the paper, or on when the examination was taken, than on what was actually written (Hopkins 1921).

The reliability problem is perhaps best illustrated by a simple example. In 1961 a study was conducted at Educational Testing Service (ETS) in which 300 essays written by college freshmen were rated by 53 readers representing several professional fields (French 1962). Each rater used a 9-point scale. The results showed that none of the 300 essays received fewer than 5 of the 9 possible ratings, 23 percent of the essays received 7 different ratings, 37 percent received 8 different ratings, and 34 percent received all possible ratings. It was clear from this study that the score received depended to a large degree on which expert happened to be doing the scoring.

The severity of the reliability problem noted was accentuated by the realization that readers represented only one source of error. Perhaps greater errors in a direct assessment are introduced by the limited sampling of topics on which students can write. Furthermore, additional errors are introduced by a tendency for errors to be correlated (because readers are influenced similarly by extraneous factors such as essay length, handwriting quality, and neatness) and by interactions among the different sources of error. The sources of reader error are many. A study by Sheppard (1929) showed dramatic variations in the scores received by identical essay responses differing only in penmanship. Of course, penmanship is probably less important today, but there is some evidence that it can still affect the score assigned to an essay examination (Markham 1976). In another early study, Traxler and Anderson (1935) showed that two independent scores assigned by experienced readers of essay examinations agreed fairly well for one essay topic but not for a second topic. It was also observed that the grades assigned to essays tended to be influenced by the grades given to the papers immediately preceding. Stalnaker (1936) noted, in this regard, that "a 'C' paper may be graded 'B' if it is read after an illiterate theme, but if it follows an 'A' paper, if such can be found, it seems to be of 'D' caliber."

The overall impact of the reliability problem manifests itself when one attempts to correlate judgmental scores of essays with external criteria for purposes of validation. More often than not, correlations of judgmental scores with other measures are lower than would be expected, and this is usually caused by the low reliability of the judgmental scores.

The College Board has commissioned a number of research studies to determine how best to assess writing skill. Huddleston (1954) collected a comprehensive set of essays from students and related them to English composition course grades, instructor judgments of student writing skill, and multiple-choice measures of verbal aptitude and composition skill. For the 763 high school students studied, an essay score was found to correlate .43 with high school English grades and .41 with high school teachers' ratings of writing ability. A multiple-choice test of English, however, correlated .60 with English grades and .58 with teachers' ratings of writing ability. Huddleston concluded that the multiple-choice measures were superior to the essay measures.

In 1961 the Godshalk study, mentioned earlier, was initiated. A total of 24 secondary schools, both public and private, collaborated. Subjects were eleventh- and twelfth-grade students in English classes. Each student wrote five free-writing exercises, and each of these five writing samples was scored by five different readers. The total of these scores was then correlated with multiple-choice test scores of several types and with scores on interlinear (editing) tasks. The highest correlations were obtained for multiple-choice usage and sentence correction tests and the lowest for multiple-choice tests of paragraph organization. The results of this investigation were later published (Godshalk, Swineford, and Coffman 1966), and this study was considered for some time the quintessential study of writing assessment. The findings of the study led to the use of multiple-choice usage and sentence correction items as the primary testing devices in the College Board's English Composition Achievement Test and in other composition tests. The Godshalk et al. study also demonstrated that brief 20-minute composition tests were useful adjuncts to multiple-choice tests.

The French study (1962), already mentioned, examined the scoring of essays by readers representing different professional fields. Several factors were identified that explained variation in the scores assigned: ideas, organization, wording, flavor. As an outcome of this analysis, Diederich (1974) developed an analytic scoring scheme that used the identified factors plus some traditional ones: usage, punctuation, spelling, handwriting.

Over the years the Diederich system has become a popular method of analytic scoring.

In the late 1970s, College Board interest in writing research turned to the new Test of Standard Written English (TSWE), a 30-minute multiple-choice test administered along with the Scholastic Aptitude Test (SAT). Although administered with the SAT, the TSWE was intended for placement in English classes—not for admissions. A research investigation of the TSWE (Breland and Gaynor 1979) showed that even a brief test of usage and sentence correction items correlated well with the scores assigned by readers on three different writing tasks collected during the course of the freshman year. As had the Godshalk et al. study, this one also demonstrated the utility of the 20-minute essay test.

In addition to the above-mentioned research sponsored either by the College Board or by Educational Testing Service, numerous research reports and papers on writing assessment have been published. This research goes back at least as far as 1880, and frequent publications on writing assessment have appeared during the last 20 years. A review of this work in Breland (1983) concluded that writing skill is inherently difficult to assess. Essay assessments were found to be often unreliable and always labor-intensive, expensive, and cumbersome. Non-essay approaches, on the other hand, lack credibility among many who teach English composition.

Despite the wealth of research on writing assessment, many questions remain. How do essay assessments of writing skill differ from non-essay assessments? How might the strengths of one best complement the weaknesses of the other? How might the costs of essay assessments be reduced? Would it be possible to integrate writing assessment with writing instruction? The questions go on, but these four have been central to this investigation and have resulted in four objectives for the project:

1. To provide a better understanding of how essay assessments of writing skills differ from multiple-choice assessments of writing skills.

2. To provide a better understanding of how these two kinds of assessment can complement one another.

3. To explore ways to reduce the cost and enhance the effectiveness of essay testing.

4. To strengthen the relationship between the assessment process and the educational process.

## 2. Description of the study

For the achievement of the study objectives, some collaboration with educational institutions was necessary. But what kinds of institutions, how many, and which ones would be best? A second set of questions related to the essay tasks to be used: how many, of what types, how administered? Once the essays were obtained, there were scoring questions: what kinds of scoring, by how many readers distributed in what way?

A critical decision that was made early in the planning phase of the study was to collaborate with postsecondary institutions rather than with secondary schools, as had been done in the Godshalk et al. (1966) study. The principal reason for this decision was that data would already be available for many students entering higher education. That is, measures of academic aptitude as well as of writing skill are routinely made during the process of application for admission. Thus, if the postsecondary institutions were chosen carefully, a wealth of data would be available: it would be necessary only to supplement these data with additional data collections made after the students entered college. The alternative possibility of working with secondary schools would not have had this advantage, since not all high school students apply to college.

Once the decision had been made to involve postsecondary institutions, the next planning task was to decide how many such institutions would be needed. It was reasoned that probably not more than two class sections of entering freshmen could easily be managed in each institution. Since it was expected that classes were nominally of about 25 students each, about 50 students might be involved in each institution. A minimum of 200 cases total was set to allow for the kinds of data analyses planned. But a special concern was that in a data collection of the type contemplated, there would be much missing data. That is, when multiple assessments of each student are to be made, it is anticipated that many students will not complete all assessment tasks and some completed tasks may not be usable because of illegibility or for other reasons. Because of the anticipated data losses, it was decided to engage six postsecondary institutions, and 50 students (nominally) in each, to obtain data for approximately 300 students. If one-third of the cases were lost because of missing data or other problems, 200 would remain as complete data cases.

Next came the determination of which six institutions to collaborate with. Of course, they would have to be interested in, and committed to, the study. Other preferences were the following:

1. The institutions should be geographically dispersed with not more than a single institution in any one state.
2. The institutions should require the Scholastic Aptitude Test as a part of the application process.
3. The institutions' students should represent a

range of abilities. For that reason it was decided that not more than one of the collaborating institutions could be highly selective.

4. The institutions should preferably require the English Composition Achievement Test of the College Board.

The process of identifying potential collaborators began early in the summer of 1984, and an initial set of 10 institutions expressed interest. Four were excluded because they were less suited for the study than were the remaining six.

## Planning conference

In August 1984 a planning conference was held among representatives of the selected institutions: Brandeis University, Rutgers University at Camden, Spelman College, Texas A&M University, the University of California at Los Angeles, and the University of Vermont. Each institution was represented by at least one member of its freshman writing program, and these representatives constituted what came to be known as the Project Working Committee. During this planning conference a number of issues were discussed. One concern was the amount of class time that could be used for the project's purposes. An agreement was reached that six essays would be written by each student, mostly in class. Two essays would be written in a narrative mode, two in an expository mode, and two in a persuasive mode.[1] The narrative essays would be written in a completely impromptu manner, with no advance notice as to topic. For the expository essays the topic would be announced in advance, but the essays would be written during 45 minutes of class time, as would the narrative essays. Each of the persuasive essays was to be a take-home task, with an initial reading assignment to intro-

duce the topic, an in-class or conference session for writing first drafts, and an in-class session for discussion of the drafts. Following this, students would take the drafts home for rewriting.

A major task during the planning conference was to choose among suggested topics submitted by members of the Project Working Committee. Most of the submitted topics had previously been used in classrooms of the six participating institutions. After considerable discussion covering the greater part of the two-day conference, six tentative tasks were identified, which were developed into those actually used in the study as described in Chapter 3 of this report.

## Data collection

The collection of data began in September 1984 with each institution following a schedule suited to its special circumstances; one institution, for example, operated on a quarter system. Data collection was completed in December 1984, except for makeup essays. All essays were available for scoring by January 1985.

Problems encountered during the data collection were not unexpected. Many students did not complete all six essays and were thus excluded from the study. Approximately 20 essays were illegible and had to be rewritten by project staff, who took care, of course, not to change language or punctuation used. In all, approximately 350 students wrote essays, but complete data were obtained for only 267 of these. Even so, this ratio of 76 percent complete data cases was better than the 67 percent planned.

## Essay scoring design

The principal method of scoring was holistic; the basic design for holistic essay scoring is presented in Table 2.1. A total of nine readers was used. The first three readers were assigned to essays written in the narrative mode, the second

---

1. Although the writing tasks were eventually classified by purpose rather than mode, the term *mode* is used here and in the data analyses as the more easily recognized and less cumbersome term.

## Table 2.1. Design for holistic essay scoring

| Student | Narrative mode | | Expository mode | | Persuasive mode | |
| --- | --- | --- | --- | --- | --- | --- |
| | Topic 1 | Topic 2 | Topic 3 | Topic 4 | Topic 5 | Topic 6 |
| S1 | R1 R2 R3 | R1 R2 R3 | R4 R5 R6 | R4 R5 R6 | R7 R8 R9 | R7 R8 R9 |
| S2 | R1 R2 R3 | R1 R2 R3 | R4 R5 R6 | R4 R5 R6 | R7 R8 R9 | R7 R8 R9 |
| S3 | R1 R2 R3 | R1 R2 R3 | R4 R5 R6 | R4 R5 R6 | R7 R8 R9 | R7 R8 R9 |
| . . . | . . . | . . . | . . . | . . . | . . . | . . . |
| S267 | R1 R2 R3 | R1 R2 R3 | R4 R5 R6 | R4 R5 R6 | R7 R8 R9 | R7 R8 R9 |

Note: Readers 1 through 9 are indicated by R1, R2, etc.

three to essays in the expository mode, and the third three to essays in the persuasive mode. Within each mode, each reader read all essays. In addition to holistic scoring, a simplified scoring design was used to conduct error counts for a sample of essays. Further details of the essay scoring procedures are given in Chapter 4.

## Measures

The six essays written by each student, when each essay was scored holistically by three different readers, produced a total of 18 holistic essay scores for each student (see Appendix A for the essay tasks). These 18 reader scores were combined to produce composite essay scores for each of the six topics and for all six topics taken together. A sample of essays was also subjected to error counts (see Appendix B). In addition to the essay scores, a number of other measures were available for analysis. Through matches with the College Board data files, six multiple-choice test scores were obtained for most students in the study. Most students also completed the Student Descriptive Questionnaire (SDQ) (see Appendix C for the wording of questions). Information was obtained from course instructors in the form of course grades and two specific ratings of student writing skills (see Appendix D for rating form and instructions and see also Appendix E, note 1). Finally, some measures were derived

from others by combining the information available. A list of the variables used in the study follows.

*Holistic scores of essays on a scale of 1 [low] to 6 [high])*
1. First narrative essay, Reader 1
2. First narrative essay, Reader 2
3. First narrative essay, Reader 3
4. Second narrative essay, Reader 1
5. Second narrative essay, Reader 2
6. Second narrative essay, Reader 3
7. First expository essay, Reader 4
8. First expository essay, Reader 5
9. First expository essay, Reader 6
10. Second expository essay, Reader 4
11. Second expository essay, Reader 5
12. Second expository essay, Reader 6
13. First persuasive essay, Reader 7
14. First persuasive essay, Reader 8
15. First persuasive essay, Reader 9
16. Second persuasive essay, Reader 7
17. Second persuasive essay, Reader 8
18. Second persuasive essay, Reader 9

*Holistic score composites*
19. Narrative one (variables 1 + 2 + 3)
20. Narrative two (variables 4 + 5 + 6)
21. Expository one (variables 7 + 8 + 9)
22. Expository two (variables 10 + 11 + 12)
23. Persuasive one (variables 13 + 14 + 15)

24. Persuasive two (variables 16 + 17 + 18)
25. Essay total (variables 19 + 20 + 21 + 22 + 23 + 24)

*Error count: grammar, usage, and sentence structure (GUSS)*
26. First narrative essay, GUSS
27. Second narrative essay, GUSS
28. First expository essay, GUSS
29. Second expository essay, GUSS
30. First persuasive essay, GUSS
31. Second persuasive essay, GUSS

*Error count: punctuation, spelling, capitalization, etc. (PSC)*
32. First narrative essay, PSC
33. Second narrative essay, PSC
34. First expository essay, PSC
35. Second expository essay, PSC
36. First persuasive essay, PSC
37. Second persuasive essay, PSC

*Error count composites*
38. First narrative total (GUSS + PSC)
39. Second narrative total (GUSS + PSC)
40. First expository total (GUSS + PSC)
41. Second expository total (GUSS + PSC)
42. First persuasive total (GUSS + PSC)
43. Second persuasive total (GUSS + PSC)
44. GUSS total (sum of variables 26–31)
45. PSC total (sum of variables 32–37)
46. Error count total (sum of variables 44 and 45)

*Multiple-choice test scores*
47. SAT-V (Scholastic Aptitude Test-verbal score)
48. SAT-M (Scholastic Aptitude Test-mathematical score)
49. SAT-Reading (Scholastic Aptitude Test-reading score)
50. SAT-Vocabulary (Scholastic Aptitude Test-vocabulary score)
51. TSWE (Test of Standard Written English)
52. ECT (English Composition Test)

*Student self-reports*
53. High school class rank (SDQ 5)
54. High school English grade (SDQ 12)
55. High school mathematics grade (SDQ 13)
56. High school foreign language grade (SDQ 14)
57. High school biology grade (SDQ 15)
58. High school physics grade (SDQ 16)
59. High school social studies grade (SDQ 17)
60. English best language (Yes/No, SDQ 38)
61. Creative writing ability (SDQ 50)
62. Written expression ability (SDQ 60)

*Instructor's ratings*
63. Course grade, on a 14-point scale from A to F using pluses and minuses
64. Discourse skills, on the same scale used for course grade
65. Mechanics skills, on the same scale used for course grade

*Derived variables*
66. HSGPA (average of variables 54–59)
67. Writing skill—instructor's judgment (variables 64 + 65)
68. Writing skill—student's judgment (variables 61 + 62)

# Samples

The samples of cases available for analysis were dependent on the availability of measures. Not all measures were available for all cases, and not all measures were of equivalent quality. The principal variable not available for all cases was the ECT, since it was not required by all institutions in the study. For two institutions this insufficiency was partially corrected by special data collections, but these required special scaling and equating procedures for which the accuracy of scaling and equating was less than it is for regular operational administrations. A final problem with the ECT measure was that some administrations—namely, the December administration of that test each year—include an essay component.

Accordingly, for analyses comparing essay and multiple-choice assessments, it is necessary either to remove the essay part of the score statistically or to use a sample that does not include an essay in the ECT score. Because of these complications with the ECT, four different samples were developed and used for different analyses.

▪ *Sample A*. This sample consisted of a total of 267 cases for which complete essay data were available and for which matches had been made with College Board files containing SAT and TSWE scores. Most of these cases also had student self-report information from the Student Descriptive Questionnaire (see Appendix E, note 2).

▪ *Sample B*. Of the 267 cases of Sample A, a total of 210 had ECT scores either from regular administrations or from special administrations conducted for this study. Those scores from special administrations required special equating and scaling procedures that were not so accurate as the regular administration procedures. Additionally, for this sample, ECT scores containing essays were corrected statistically to remove the contribution of the essay from the score (see Appendix E, note 3).

▪ *Sample C*. This sample was also drawn from Sample A. It comprised 141 cases for which regular reported ECT scores were available. Thus, no special equating or scaling operations were required to produce ECT scores. No statistical procedures were used to remove essay scores. In summary, this sample had complete data including ECT scores as reported from regular administrations. Approximately one-third of the reported scores, however, included a 20-minute essay component (see Appendix E, note 4).

▪ *Sample D*. A total of 94 cases had ECT scores based entirely on a 60-minute multiple-choice test. The scores available were the same scores developed from regular administration scaling and equating procedures and reported to students and institutions. In summary, these ECT scores were the best scores for use in comparing multiple-choice and essay modes of writing skill assessment (see Appendix E, note 5).

Table 2.2 presents a comparison of these samples with 1984 college-bound seniors taken from Arbeiter (1984). In terms of SAT-verbal scores and TSWE scores, Table 2.2 shows that all four samples are above the national average. But when compared on ECT scores, all four samples are below the national average. Standard deviations for all four samples are somewhat below those for the national sample. It seems likely that students attending the participating institutions were admitted on the basis of test scores, and as a consequence one would expect the SAT-verbal and the TSWE means to be higher than means for all students. Moreover, it is likely that test scores were used to place students in freshman English courses, and such a use of tests would further reduce the standard deviations for students in samples A through D.

## Table 2.2. Comparison of samples

| Sample | Mean scores | | | Standard deviations | | |
|---|---|---|---|---|---|---|
| | SAT-V | TSWE | ECT | SAT-V | TSWE | ECT |
| 1984 college-bound seniors[a] | 426 | 42.6 | 518 | 110 | 10.9 | 102 |
| Sample A (267) | 443 | 45.4 | — | 85 | 8.0 | — |
| Sample B (210) | 447 | 45.7 | 451 | 87 | 8.0 | 78 |
| Sample C (141) | 459 | 47.0 | 471 | 81 | 7.9 | 77 |
| Sample D ( 94) | 462 | 46.6 | 467 | 89 | 8.8 | 80 |

a. Figures are based on 964,684 students with SAT-V scores, 964,676 students with TSWE scores, and 183,639 students with ECT scores.

## 3. Development and administration of the writing tasks

As noted in Chapter 1, the 1966 study *The Measurement of Writing Ability* used as the criterion of writing performance a collection of five writing samples per student. The five topics used to elicit those samples varied considerably in the demands they made on the student writer. Three of the papers were to be written in 20 minutes, two in 40 minutes. Of the 20-minute topics, one called for a description in the letter genre addressed to a specific but remote audience. The second asked for an "imaginative story," a narrative about an experience or an object. The third asked for an essentially expository essay on an arguable position. The two 40-minute topics involved judgments about the character of students in school-related contexts but called for different kinds of writing—the first a defense of a selected course of action and the second an analysis of character based on a brief talk. In all, then, the collection included one description, one narration, one expository paper with an argumentative focus, one persuasive paper with elements of problem solving, and one analysis. Though various and therefore likely to yield a desirable range of writing experiences, the topics did not lend themselves to any clear grouping on the basis of rhetorical demand.

## *Determining the kinds of tasks to be included*

Research and instruction in the years since 1966 (Moffett 1968; Kinneavy 1971; Britton 1975) have enhanced considerably our awareness of distinctions among the purposes for writing and, more recently, among the demands made on writers by various kinds of writing tasks (Ruth and Keech 1982; Ruth and Murphy 1984, 1986; Witte et al. forthcoming). It seemed essential that the present study reflect this awareness in the design of its criterion. It seemed equally important that the study be designed so that variance in measurement arising from a specific topic could be distinguished from variance attributable to the purpose for writing. For these reasons the criterion was designed to make clear distinctions between the purposes for writing and to present two topics for each purpose.

Since the value of the study would depend to a large extent on how well the criterion represented students' overall writing ability, it was important that the writing samples cover as full a range of performances in writing as possible. Practical considerations, however, suggested that the total number of writing samples be kept within manageable limits. In addition, the need for high reliability in the criterion meant that it would be necessary to exercise some degree of control over the conditions in which students wrote their papers, a procedure likely to intrude more heavily on classroom objectives for course work with a large number of samples.

The results of an earlier project (Camp 1983, 1985) suggested a reasonable compromise. In that project, which explored a portfolio method of assessing writing ability, information was gathered from teachers of writing and refined by teachers and researchers to create a manageable but comprehensive sampling of student writing performance. The major components of that sampling were papers written for three distinct purposes under semicontrolled classroom conditions. Together the three papers were believed to constitute a sample of writing performance sufficiently comprehensive to illustrate the repertoire of skills and abilities most essential to the writing of twelfth graders and college freshmen. If sufficient attention were given to the rhetorical demands of each of the topics, the papers would also cover the domain described by current taxonomies for writing.

Drawing on this experience, we believed that the criterion in the present study would be reasonably comprehensive in its representation of student writing ability, as well as efficient and reliable, if we could collect classroom-generated samples for carefully designed topics in each of three writing purposes: narrative, expository, and persuasive. We therefore designed the study so that students would write on a total of six topics in their regular first-semester composition courses. Two topics, comparable in the demands they made on the writers, would be designed to elicit writing directed toward each of the three purposes. Each pair of topics would be presented under the same conditions from one classroom to another.

Another element was necessary to the design, however, if the writing samples were to constitute a sound and representative basis for judgments about student writing performance. In the years since 1966, increasing emphasis on the writing process and on the audience addressed in writing had become evident in research and instruction (Moffett 1968; Emig 1971; Kinneavy 1971; Britton 1975; Perl 1980; Sommers 1980; Faigley and Witte 1981; Flower and Hayes 1981). Our experience with the portfolio project had indicated, in fact, that a representative collection of writing samples would include some writing done over a period of time, under circumstances allowing for thought and process in the development of the writing, and some writing addressed to a specified audience.

Believing that the data collection would not be sufficiently controlled if all six topics allowed students to work on their papers outside the classroom, we decided that only one pair of topics would make direct provision for process in the writing. This decision meant some loss of comparability among the conditions for writing on the three sets of topics but a clear gain in the validity of the criterion without much sacrifice in control over conditions.

The topics for which a process approach seemed most promising were those calling for persuasive writing. In comparison with other purposes for writing, the persuasive purpose seemed most likely to be enhanced by presentation in a context involving thinking and writing in advance of the final draft. Similarly, the purpose of persuasion seemed to have greater integrity if the writing was to be addressed to a particular audience.

The sampling procedure also affected our requirements for the topics. As noted in Chapter 2, the students in the study who were to write the six papers in their first-semester writing courses would represent a full range of verbal ability and academic interests, and the institutions would represent as far as possible a diversity of colleges and universities. For this procedure to work well, the topics for the study would need to be equally appropriate to all of these students. They would have to be accessible to students at the low end of the range and challenging to students at the high end; further, they would need to engage the interest of students with a variety of backgrounds and experiences in different parts of the country.

## Process of development

For six topics to be presented to students in a comparable manner in six different freshman writing programs would also require a high degree of understanding and cooperation on the part of participating teachers. The teachers, we realized, would need to feel sufficiently comfortable with the writing tasks and with the rationale behind them to integrate them into the course work for the term. In this sense, the teachers would need to feel that the topics were their own. For this reason the project collaborators were asked to work with us in the creation of mutually acceptable topics and a workable procedure for collecting the data.

As indicated in Chapter 2, the six teachers of writing, who were also directors or assistant directors of writing programs, were to meet with us in August 1984 to discuss the design of the criterion and to generate a set of six topics to be used in their writing courses in the fall term. In the meantime, each sent us three possible topics for writing samples to be included in the criterion, one topic for each of the three kinds of writing to be elicited. We classified topics by the purpose of the writing called for, looked for possible pairings of topics on the basis of demands within each purpose, and rounded out the collection by adding topics from our own files of pretested topics. We sent all the topics to teacher-researchers who had done considerable work investigating the relationships between topic design and student performance. They identified the topics they believed most likely to yield scorable responses exhibiting the purposes for writing wanted for the study and indicated possible pairings of topics with comparable rhetorical demands. For the most promising topics they also suggested refor-mulations that would increase the likelihood of our getting scorable responses with the desired purpose.

At the August conference our discussion with the teacher-collaborators led to some modification of the design for the criterion and some refocusing of the objectives for the project. Our earlier concerns with control in the data collection were alleviated by the collaborators' indications that the classroom setting and the process orientation of their writing courses made it extremely unlikely that students could have others fulfill their writing assignments for them. The orientation of their writing courses, however, made necessary more accommodations to process than we had anticipated for the writing samples. After some discussion we decided that the following arrangement was best for the teachers and for the project:

- Two narrative/descriptive papers written early in the semester in response to impromptu topics (45 minutes).
- Two expository papers written in response to topics presented near the end of the previous class period. These papers could be used as the basis for further drafts, but the first-draft, in-class responses would be collected for the research project (45 minutes).
- Two persuasive papers written in, and guided by, a four-step process:
1. Students receive reading material acquainting them with contrasting arguments on an issue. They read the material and think about the issue in preparation for writing (at-home assignment).
2. Students are given a topic designed to help them focus on the issue and address an appropriate audience in their first drafts, which they write during the class period. Drafts are collected and duplicated; one copy is sent in for the project (45 minutes).
3. Students' first drafts (or copies) are returned to them accompanied by some form of teacher or peer review.

4. Approximately two weeks after writing the first drafts, students turn in typed final drafts revised as they think appropriate in light of the earlier review. These drafts (or copies) are collected for the research project (two weeks).

By the end of the conference we had selected six topics that were appropriate for the research design and for the conditions established for presentation of the topics and were acceptable to the project collaborators for use in their writing programs. We had decided on the actual text for some of the topics, although others would need further revision and review. The comparability of topics within the pairs, while not exact, was thought to be reasonably good.

There followed a series of reviews and revisions by ETS subject-matter specialists in writing assessment. For the second persuasive topic it was necessary to follow through on the conference decisions by collecting material on the specified issue and formulating the topic in terms comparable with those already worked out for the first persuasive topic. All topics were then submitted to rigorous reviews by consultants and were revised again in response to those reviews.

## Issues in the development of writing tasks

Recent research into the characteristics of essay topics has led to increased awareness of the ways in which the formulation of topics affects writing performance (Ruth and Keech 1982; Ruth and Murphy 1984, 1986; White 1985; Witte et al. forthcoming). In the development of the six topics for the project's writing samples, a number of concerns became apparent, many of them related to issues raised by previous research. Some concerns were common to the development of all carefully designed prompts for writing. These we addressed by the traditional methods: careful analysis and review based on prior experience with the topic itself and on accumulated knowl-

edge about the performance of writers addressing similar topics. Other concerns, however, derived from the design of the particular group of writing samples needed for the criterion and from the circumstances in which the topics would be presented and the papers written.

The decision to include writing for three purposes was a major step toward ensuring the comprehensiveness of the criterion, especially since the purposes chosen represented the varieties of writing most important to students of the age group in the study. For the criterion writing samples to effectively cover the domain of writing abilities described by current taxonomies, however, more would be required. We had found we could avoid entanglement in the conflicts among taxonomies by focusing on purposes for writing rather than on modes or genre as such, but within those purposes we would need to design topics whose rhetorical demands would call for a range of writing ability common to several taxonomies. We also realized that the decision to maintain clear distinctions among the purposes for writing would have to be carried out in a manner consistent with our recognition that real-world and even school-based writing nearly always combines purposes. Especially for the first two pairs of topics, we knew that writing that was entirely pure in its purpose would be unrepresentative of the writing experience of twelfth-grade and first-year-college students.

Given these considerations, it seemed reasonable that the three purposes for writing should be understood in terms providing for the broadest possible sampling of student writing ability and the best representation of those purposes as understood in other contexts for writing. Our selection and refinement of the topics were guided by these motives, which are expressed in the following set of criteria describing the kinds of writing to be elicited:

1. The purpose of the narrative/descriptive writing is the presentation of personal experience—

the recounting of autobiographical information. It is closest to inner speech and to expression intended for the self or for a trusted other; it is less discursive than is either expository or persuasive writing.

2. The purpose of the expository writing is to set forth an idea—to inform and explain. The topic should be formulated so that the writing will include analysis and so that the idea to be set forth will involve some observations about the world or the society. In this way the writer will be moved toward a public arena for writing—toward writing that involves interaction with others, writing that is transactional.

3. The purpose of the persuasive writing is to convince others that they should share the writer's view on the issue under discussion. The topic should be formulated to elicit writing that is clearly transactional and whose intention is to accomplish a change in the world or in others' perceptions of the world. It will be set up to evoke the analysis of problems and issues and the proposal of appropriate solutions.

Since the reason for using two topics for each writing purpose was to distinguish effects arising from topic from those arising from purpose, and since the content of a particular topic appears to be a strong variable in writing performance, affecting both the writer's engagement with the topic and the details and evidence necessary to the paper's development, we attempted to make the paired topics as similar as possible in all respects.

For each topic within a pair we drew on subjects with approximately the same degree of interest for the age group in the study. Within each pair we also looked for subjects from the same general arena of human activity, believing that the writing should draw as far as possible on the same kind of knowledge and experience for each topic within a pair. The wording of the topics aimed at comparable rhetorical tasks presented in the same sequence in each pair. We recognized that no two topics can be made exactly equivalent in their demands on the writer, but we attempted to limit those differences insofar as it was possible without impairing the integrity of the individual topics.

The development of the topics was both enriched and complicated by the need to provide for their presentation in a classroom setting. The dynamic between expectations for classroom-generated writing and the controls necessary for comparability of data was evident throughout the development process. We had the advantage of being able to incorporate elements of the writing process and to call for a range of skills not traditionally seen in large-scale assessment. We also found, however, that the more thoroughly writing tasks were to be integrated with instruction, the more difficult they became to develop. The conflict between the desire for pedagogical intervention and for comparability of data became more intense with the greater number of topics and the greater complexity of the tasks they presented.

As might be expected, the development of topics was more complicated for prompts accommodating process in writing. These prompts were immediately made more cumbersome because each stage in the process required a separate set of materials. For each of the two persuasive tasks we provided the following:

1. A description in general terms of the writing assignment as a whole, an introduction to the issue to be addressed, and reading material setting out alternative perspectives on the issue.

2. A prompt giving a focus for the issue and a basis for writing a first draft.

3. An assignment sheet describing the procedure for creating and turning in the final draft.

4. Instructions for teachers setting out the agreed-on sequence of writing activities and procedures for teacher and/or peer evaluation of the first drafts.

The formulation of each of these four components required the resolution of tensions between part and whole or instruction and assessment. Each step in the sequence needed to have integrity in itself but also to be seen as leading in due course to the completion of the assignment as a whole. The reading material and the accompanying introduction to the issue were to provide a base of information and to stimulate ideas about a variety of perspectives on the issue, but they could not be allowed to overwhelm even the least accomplished writers. The prompt for the first draft was to provide some focus for the writing but not restrict it. The creation of the final draft had to allow for genuine process, including peer review and discussion, but the conditions in which it was created needed to be roughly comparable from one student to another and from one classroom to another.

Similarly, topics became more difficult to develop to the extent that they asked students to engage with an audience different from the teacher-evaluator audience for which they write in most conventional assessments. For the narrative/descriptive and expository topics, we asked students to write to an audience made up of their classmates and teacher. We hoped in this way to give them the sense of an audience more immediate and less formal than the conventional teacher-as-evaluator. For the persuasive topics, however, we wanted students to write to an audience more integral to the purpose and subject of the topics. In an early version of the first persuasive topic, we established a hypothetical context for the entire writing assignment much like those used in case study composition textbooks (Field and Weiss 1984; Tedlock and Jarvie 1981). The reviews, however, by ETS subject-matter specialists and consulting teacher-researchers showed dissatisfaction with this approach, pointing out the problems likely to arise from the students' perception of a discrepancy between the hypothetical audience and the audience of teachers and classmates who would respond to the writing.

Because these objections coincide with concerns of our own, we decided on a more straightforward approach to audience. Students were told early in the assignment sequence that the response for their first drafts would come from their teachers and classmates but that they would be encouraged to send the completed final drafts to policymakers who could effect the solutions they proposed. They would thus have the opportunity both to try out their ideas on a familiar audience near at hand and to address an appropriate real-world audience when their drafts were completed, though they would not be required to send out their final drafts.

This procedure resolved the problem of immediate versus hypothetical audience, but it required that for each topic we locate genuine audiences interested in the views of students in different geographic regions. After some research we were able to suggest specific audiences at local, state, and federal levels for the two issues presented in the topics and to provide names and addresses for the appropriate policymakers at the state and federal levels. Since we could not be as specific in naming local policymakers, we described them and their functions and indicated where their names and addresses could be obtained.

Independent of the challenges created by incorporating purpose and audience in two of the writing tasks, the three pairs of topics raised different kinds of issues in their development. For the narrative/descriptive writing, although the large number of subjects available from personal experience seemed to suggest that topic development would be an easy matter, many subjects were discovered to be too personal or too specialized for presentation to a diverse group of students. Further, the topics needed to be framed so that the writing would have a clear direction or point and so that all students responding to them would have the same expectations about genre. We believed that narrative topics that were not carefully formulated could yield responses ranging from pure storytelling to generalized narrative or illustration of a point by means of separately described events. Such variety in genre would make the evaluation of the papers more difficult.

The topics for expository writing were easiest to develop, probably because these kinds of topics are most common in both instruction and assessment. They draw on the many areas of interest in which student experience can become the basis for generalizations or observations about a larger social context. Comparatively few of the potential subjects are likely to elicit writing that is either too personal or too abstract; many are within the arena of public discourse most conducive to the evaluation of writing. In selecting and revising expository topics, the major challenge was to provide sufficient motivation for the writing while maintaining the expository purpose as primary. The topics that were developed ask for observation, analysis, and generalization in the writing itself, but on subjects for which such expository writing could well lead to expression of opinion. Exposition remains the primary focus, but the issues raised by the subject are sufficiently compelling to give point to the writing.

Inherent in the selection of subject matter for any writing prompt is a conflict between motivating the writer's engagement and encouraging objectivity. A subject that has no compelling interest for the writer generates perfunctory writing, whereas a subject that is too compelling evokes emotionally unbalanced responses. This conflict becomes most acute in topics designed to elicit persuasive writing from young people. We believed we could resolve the conflict in the persuasive topics by presenting issues affecting the lives of students in the age group in the sample but avoiding issues likely to involve religious or political controversy. We also believed it was important to present the issues in a way that would promote genuine engagement and response but would lead beyond the sometimes emotional, sometimes self-centered first response of young writers toward a more reasoned public stance. Fortunately, the three-step presentation of the topics provided a context in which we could do so.

A second concern was related to the problem of engagement versus objectivity. We had observed that topics intended to evoke persuasive writing often put young writers in the position of expressing opinions without having sufficient information either to arrive at or to support them intelligently. Since we were not constrained by the time limits of most traditional assessments, we were able to provide information and conflicting perspectives on the issues and possible approaches to thinking about them. By suggesting to students the richness of the issues involved and possible connections with the students' own experience, the topic materials gave students a reasonable opportunity to demonstrate their abilities as writers of persuasive prose. In an impromptu topic, that opportunity could not easily be provided.

A third concern in the development of the persuasive topics was possible differences in students' expectations about genre. It is difficult to design prompts that compensate for these differences, since they are related to the writers' individual decisions about how they wish to engage their audience. Those writers who choose to frame their argument in terms that would appeal to any educated person will write responses that look very much like academic papers. A student who is keenly aware of the effectiveness of appealing to the particular interests of a particular audience will write something more like a letter or a newspaper column. We did not attempt to restrict this diversity of responses because we had decided not to require students' direct engagement with their real-world audience, but the issue should be considered by others developing prompts for persuasive writing.

Comparisons of the effort involved in developing the three kinds of prompts cannot be absolute, since the materials we started with at the end of the conference were in various states of completeness. Nevertheless, some comparisons can be made. Topics designed to evoke expository writing were easiest to develop. Topics for narrative/descriptive writing required more care than was at first apparent, perhaps because we had less experience with the effects of topic design on writing performance for this kind of writing. Some of the complications we experienced, such as those arising from the conflict between engagement and objectivity, can be attributed to our decision to incorporate process and audience in these topics. Others, though, appear to be inherent in the development of persuasive topics as such; some, in fact, may be easier to resolve in a context involving process and audience than in a context that does not.

## Presentation of writing tasks and collection of writing samples

At the end of the conference we had agreed with the teacher-collaborators on a procedure for introducing the research project to their students, presenting the writing tasks, and collecting the writing samples. That procedure, with some later refinement of details, ensured the comparability among classrooms that we considered necessary to the project. We also knew that the teachers participating in the project would be acting out of a shared sense of the purpose of the project and of the six writing tasks. For the sake of comparability they had agreed to present the tasks in the same order and in roughly the same instructional context in their classrooms. They were equally strong in their commitment to a process orientation for the persuasive writing tasks, though they differed somewhat in their preferences for teacher or peer review of first drafts, a difference we felt tolerable. For our part, we were to follow through on the development and refinement of the writing tasks and to send the completed materials to the participating institutions according to the agreed-on procedure.

During this phase of the project the following materials were sent to each of the participating institutions: a letter describing the project to students and asking their consent, instructions for presenting the writing tasks, six writing tasks in booklets with space for writing, additional instructions for the persuasive topics, and extra booklets and blank pages for unforeseen contingencies. We received from each institution the papers written by students on each of the six topics, including first and final drafts for persuasive writing.

## 4. Essay scoring procedures

Two distinctly different approaches were taken in scoring the essays. First, a traditional holistic scoring was conducted as a gauge of the overall quality of each essay. Second, counts were made of specific errors identified in a sample of essays. It was believed that these two approaches would capture most of the explainable variance in essay quality. Since each type of scoring was conducted by different groups of readers with several months between readings, there was no possibility that one type of scoring influenced the other.

Further details on the scoring procedures are given in the following sections.

## *Holistic scoring*

The chief assumption that underlies holistic scoring of essays is that the whole text or composition is more than the sum of its parts. To look at a composition from the aspect of its mechanics, its rhetorical structure, its syntactic patterns or complexity, or its handwriting is to view it narrowly. To look at a composition as a whole in order to judge its quality as an entity in itself is to score it holistically. When the number of compositions to be scored is large, holistic scoring is the most practical method. For that reason it is most often used in large-scale assessments.

For each of the six essays a scoring guide was developed and then used to train the readers to come to scale. The scoring scale was from 1 (low) to 6 (high). Sample papers illustrating each of the points on the scale were used to orient the readers to the sample and to the scale. Professional staff from Educational Testing Service with long experience in diverse scoring procedures first scanned the entire sample of papers. Papers were set aside that were judged to be accurate models of the score points. Consensus among staff was achieved on about 80 percent of the papers read. Discussion and analysis among staff yielded a set of 15 to 20 papers that would serve as models for the training of the readers. Using these model papers as benchmarks for the scale points, ETS staff developed scoring guides that described the quality of the writing in each paper on the scale of 1 to 6. The descriptions attempted to characterize the salient features of the text for samples in each of the score categories.

The students' essays were grouped in random order in folders of about 25 essays each. Scores were recorded on a separate sheet that stayed with the folder during the scoring by each of the readers. When a reader finished a folder, the scoring sheet was removed before the next reader scored the papers, and the order of the papers was scrambled. At the beginning of each reading, the readers were given the exercise and discussed the design and purpose of the question as well as the demands of the tasks it presented to the students. After discussion readers were given the scoring guides and discussed them in terms of the question and then in terms of the model papers, a set of eight that they rank-ordered from 6 to 1. More model papers followed until the readers felt comfortable with the scale and with the scoring guide. When the readers became more comfortable with the scale and with their judgments of the papers, they revised the scoring guide to fit their perceptions of the papers. As the reading proceeded, they found the scoring guide less useful and finally unnecessary. Thus, the scoring guides were used not as fixed directives to be followed precisely but rather as initial suggestions to be modified by readers as they accumulated experience with a topic.

The actual readings were conducted over a period of several weeks. Nine different readers worked at the task. In teams of three, they each read every essay independently within mode; that is, the two narrative essays were read by the same three readers, the two expository essays were read by a second team of three readers, and so forth. The readers were required to make their judgments about what scores to assign papers only on the basis of their experience, the training they had been given on the topic, and the scoring guides. Once consensus had been achieved in the training, no group discussion was allowed except as directed by ETS staff for the analysis of the sample papers, the occasional maverick paper, or the off-topic paper. No adjudication of divergent scores was conducted. Scores were simply totaled, so that the top score a paper could receive was 18 and the lowest score was 3.

Frequent quality checks were conducted by ETS staff who were present, and new sample or model papers were periodically given to the readers, scored, and discussed. The readers were all experienced college English teachers who taught mostly freshman English courses. The time originally scheduled for reading was one day per topic for the narrative and expository papers and two days per topic for the persuasive papers. The persuasive papers were generally longer and usually typed; they had been written over a period of weeks. The reading of the expository papers was completed in the one day per topic originally scheduled, but the narrative and persuasive papers required an extra half day per topic. The time required for readers to arrive at consensus varied from 1 hour for the expository topics to 1.5 hours for the narrative and persuasive topics. The readers were given frequent breaks to reduce fatigue and increase reliability. Excluding the initial training period, narrative papers were completed at an average rate of 33 papers per hour, expository papers at 46 papers per hour, and persuasive papers at 17 papers per hour.

## Issues raised in holistic scoring

The expository papers were scored more easily and more quickly than either the narrative/descriptive or the persuasive papers. The expository topics asked for the kind of writing most common in instruction and assessment and therefore most familiar to students and teachers in first-year college writing courses. Student expectations for the genre of expository writing are fairly well defined and widely shared. They also match closely the expectations of readers experienced in instruction and assessment in first-year college writing programs.

The first of the expository topics fell easily within the expectations for expository writing familiar to the writers and scorers of the papers. It asked for the identification of one or more current status symbols and an analysis of their appeal, a combination of tasks that involved a straightforward approach to thinking and writing consistent with students' day-to-day experience.

The second expository topic posed greater challenges for both writers and scorers. It presented tasks that were similar to those of the first topic; it asked that the writer identify articles representative of our time and culture and explain what they signify. The stipulation, however, that the articles were to be placed in a cornerstone for future discovery appeared to require an imaginative leap unfamiliar to at least some student writers. The students' responses indicated that they found the challenge of making that leap an interesting one. Many of their selections for the cornerstone were ingenious, and the writing seemed highly motivated. Nevertheless, the cleverness shown in selecting the objects did not always correspond to other writing skills to the extent that readers expected. In this regard the ingenuity of the initial conception in some papers seemed at odds with demonstrated ability to express and develop it, a disparity that made judgments of overall quality more difficult.

The second expository topic also led to somewhat greater variety in the kinds of writing elicited. Some writers focused on the implied hypothetical situation of a future generation's discovering the cornerstone. Of these writers, most then used that situation for an expository paper. Others of this group, however, made the situation the basis for an essentially narrative paper. For some, this strategy proved to be a disadvantage. The tasks of setting up the fictional context and of generating probable events left them with insufficient time for the full development of the paper.

The scoring of papers on the narrative/descriptive topics was somewhat more difficult and time-consuming than the scoring of expository papers. The discussion among the readers suggested that the criteria for effective presentational writing are more elusive than those for expository writing. There appears to be less agreement among writers and among readers about the characteristics of effective writing of this kind. In fact, a degree of flexibility seemed called for in the scoring. Since writers can be expected to use different approaches to autobiographical writing, depending on the incident or the story to be related and their own sense of effective presentation, the readers felt obliged to adapt their criteria accordingly. To do otherwise would have been to deny the writers their legitimate authority over the writing.

So that a common purpose could be established for the writing, the narrative/descriptive topics asked that events from personal experience be described in such a way as to make their significance clear to the reader. Even among papers on the same topics, the student writers responded to this requirement with varying proportions of description and commentary; some relied strictly or primarily on narrative to convey the significance of the experience, while others were more inclined to explicit commentary. Some of these differences were more pronounced across topics and could be attributed to differences in the topics. Others, however, occurred among the papers on the same topic and appear to have been derived from considerations inherent in this kind of writing. There seems to be little that could have been done in the design of the narrative/descriptive topics to ensure greater control over possible responses without imposing artificial constraints on the writing. Some events in some individuals' lives and some writers' perceptions of events carry clear implicit messages about significance, but other events and other perspectives call for explicit articulation of the perceived meaning. After scoring and discussing a number of sample papers, the readers were able to accommodate these differences in making their judgments, but they continued to believe that the differences increased the difficulties of scoring.

Because the narrative/descriptive topics were formulated in the context of personal experience, the writers had little difficulty finding material for their papers. Many of the papers were long and richly detailed; the writers appeared to be engaged and comfortable with the writing task. The topics' bases in personal experience, however, created additional demands for evaluation. The first had to do with objectivity. The experiences described in papers of this kind may be more or less interesting or compelling for reasons of personal history rather than writing ability. Events that are in themselves unusual or dramatic, especially those that call for a sympathetic response, are likely to strain the readers' objectivity in assigning scores. The second demand had to do with the difficulty of anticipating the direction for development of the paper. The direction apparent at the beginning of narrative/descriptive papers does not seem to control their development to the extent that the organization established at the beginning of expository papers controls theirs: an unanticipated event in what is presented may result in an unexpected turn in the paper's development. The readers found that those two characteristics of personal experience papers required that they be especially attentive in reading and scoring the papers.

Of the two narrative/descriptive topics, the readers preferred the second. The first asks for a description of traditions or customs shared with family or friends. Because the papers as a group tended to focus on a limited number of holidays or special occasions, the readers found considerable repetition in theme from one paper to another. The second topic, which asks for a description of a significant event or turning point in the writer's life, produced a greater variety of responses. These papers required greater attention to unexpected turns of event and tolerance for the unconsciously superior tone sometimes adopted by young people who believe they have discovered the answer to one of life's problems. Nevertheless, the readers found the papers interesting, varied in approach, and fairly typical of presentational writing for this age group.

The persuasive papers were considerably more difficult to score than either the expository or the narrative/descriptive papers. Scoring them required more time and greater concentration from the readers than is necessary for scoring papers on most topics. The readers needed more time for discussion of sample papers and more frequent breaks to alleviate fatigue.

In part the increased demands on the readers were a function of the circumstances in which the papers had been written. The topics presented considerable information on a problem that does not lend itself to easy solution; the writers were asked to evaluate the perspectives on the problem and to arrive at their own solution on the basis of the information and arguments presented. They were given time to assimilate the information, to arrive at a solution, and to reflect on what they had written in their first drafts. As a result, the papers they wrote were long, averaging three and a half to four typed pages each. They were dense in the amount of information they presented and the arguments they developed. This length and density made it difficult for readers to hold in mind the impressions of writing quality they were accumulating in the process of reading a paper.

In addition, the persuasive purpose itself made further demands on the readers. To maintain objectivity, the readers found it necessary to some extent to separate their evaluation of the effectiveness of the writing from their personal response to the writer's argumentative stance and proposed solution to the problem. They also found it necessary to evaluate the papers in terms of a variety of rhetorical strategies, since these varied from paper to paper, depending on how the writer decided to define and address the audience. Some papers were rhetorically pointed and concise, whereas others were elaborated and more abstract. Some writers chose a journalistic style for their papers; others were more erudite or philosophical in approach. Some wrote a letter or an editorial; others wrote something more like a traditional academic paper.

After considerable discussion of papers in the training period and early in the reading, the readers arrived at a solid basis of consensus from which they felt secure in their judgments of the persuasive papers. Yet the scoring throughout required a high degree of concentration in reading the papers and in most cases a second glance at the paper just read in order to summarize the impressions first gathered from it.

In the persuasive mode the readers preferred the first topic, on drinking and driving, to the second, on school censorship of books. The student writers appeared to be more immediately engaged with the first topic; they seemed to find the issues of the second topic more abstract, further removed from their immediate interests. Among the papers on the second topic, those that exhibited greater commitment appeared to the readers to be consistently better and of somewhat different quality than papers whose writers were less committed. Perhaps because the development of papers on this topic did not follow inherently from the positions the writers established at the beginning of the papers, the degree of rhetorical focus that writers created for their papers appeared to determine the extent to which they were able to control the organization as they developed and supported their positions.

## Error counts

The second approach used in scoring the essays was to make error counts in six areas:
1. Grammar
2. Usage/diction
3. Sentence structure
4. Punctuation
5. Spelling
6. Capitalization, titles, contractions, etc.
Because of the time consumed in this type of scoring, only the smallest sample of 94 cases was used, and only two readers read each essay.

The error-count scoring was conducted for the 564 sampled essays by a total of 15 readers in a one-day session. Since each essay was read twice, a total of 1,128 readings was made. Each reader, therefore, read about 75 essays during the day. With 6.5 working hours (excluding training and breaks), the reading rate was slightly fewer than 12 essays per hour on the average. An analysis of error counts revealed substantial discrepancies for some papers, and as a result a third reading of these papers was conducted and error counts were adjudicated (the most discrepant count was discarded).

Forms and instructions for the error counts are given in Appendix B.

# 5. Reliabilities of the essay assessments

Reliability has always been the Achilles heel of essay assessment. It relates to the consistency of scores obtained when the same examinee takes the same test on different occasions. In other words, reliability estimates serve as indices of the likelihood that a person taking a test a second time will make the same score. Anastasi (1982, p. 399) makes this observation about the reliability of essay assessments:

*To obtain an adequate and reliable assessment of an individual's performance on essay questions— and especially an index of his or her ability to write clearly and correctly—one needs several essays on different topics, written on different days, and preferably read by different examiners.*

As described in the preceding chapters, we have followed the above advice and collected samples of student writing on six different topics. None of the essays were written on the same day, but were spread over the duration of a course in freshman English. Each of the samples was scored by three readers. As a result, we would expect to have achieved an adequate assessment of these students' writing abilities, at least as writing ability is defined in freshman college courses in English composition.

Estimates of the reliability obtained can be made by a number of methods, all of which recognize that error in the assessment comes from one or more sources. For the essay assessments of this study the potential sources of error are the examinees, the six specific topics, the three modes of discourse, and the nine readers who scored the essays. The examinees are sources of error because changes may occur in a student's condition (for example, illness, fatigue, emotional strain) between the time of one examination and the next. The specific essay topics are sources of error because an examinee may or may not know the subject matter of any given topic or may or may not have had recent experience writing about a given topic. The modes of discourse are potential sources of error because an examinee may not be familiar with the mode of discourse required by a particular task. The modes are not sources of error, however, if the modes examined are assumed to cover the entire domain of interest. The readers are sources of error because their judgments will differ on the quality of any given piece of writing.

## Correlational estimates of reliability

The actual computation of reliability coefficients is performed through various procedures, some more accurate than others. A common kind of reliability estimate made for essay assessments is the correlation between the scores assigned by different readers to the same piece of writing. Such estimates are inflated because they recognize only one source of error—the readers. Table 5.1 presents estimates of reader reliabilities based on correlations of scores assigned by different readers to the same essays. For example, in the narrative mode, the first narrative essay as scored by Reader 1 was correlated with the score assigned by Reader 2 to the same essay, and the result was a correlation of .578. Next, Reader 1's score was correlated with Reader 3's score, and then Reader 2's score was correlated with Reader 3's score. The average of these three reader score correlations was .520; this represents an estimate of the reliability of the first narrative essay when read by a single reader. Estimates for two and three readers are often "stepped up" by using the Spearman-Brown formula (see Appendix E, note 6). Since these reader reliabilities ignore sources of error other than reader error, they tend to be inflated.

Table 5.2 shows estimates of reliability based on correlations across topics within modes. These correlations represent an estimate of the reliability of a single essay read by a single reader. Averaging across the six estimates given in Table 5.2 for narrative essays yields an overall estimate of .366. The estimates for the expository and persuasive essay assessments were made similarly. The higher reliabilities for expository and persuasive essays are not necessarily a result of a superiority of these essay types, since different readers were used within type. Additionally there are possible confoundings of the order of writing and the position of an essay within the course of instruction, because the narrative essays were written early in the course and the persuasive essays near the completion of the course.

## Table 5.1. Correlational estimates of reader reliabilities (Sample A)

| Essay topic | Scores correlated | | $r$ | Reader reliability estimates for | | |
| | | | | 1 reader (average) | 2 readers | 3 readers |
|---|---|---|---|---|---|---|
| Narrative 1 | N1R1 vs. N1R2 | | .578 | .520 | .684 | .765 |
| | N1R1 vs. N1R3 | | .524 | | | |
| | N1R2 vs. N1R3 | | .458 | | | |
| Narrative 2 | N2R1 vs. N2R2 | | .568 | .517 | .682 | .762 |
| | N2R1 vs. N2R3 | | .506 | | | |
| | N2R1 vs. N2R3 | | .476 | | | |
| Expository 1 | E1R1 vs. E1R2 | | .588 | .616 | .762 | .828 |
| | E1R1 vs. E1R3 | | .637 | | | |
| | E1R2 vs. E1R3 | | .622 | | | |
| Expository 2 | E2R1 vs. E2R2 | | .610 | .599 | .749 | .818 |
| | E2R1 vs. E2R3 | | .620 | | | |
| | E2R2 vs. E2R3 | | .568 | | | |
| Persuasive 1 | P1R1 vs. P1R2 | | .676 | .651 | .789 | .848 |
| | P1R1 vs. P1R3 | | .593 | | | |
| | P1R2 vs. P1R3 | | .684 | | | |
| Persuasive 2 | P2R1 vs. P2R2 | | .675 | .597 | .748 | .816 |
| | P2R1 vs. P2R3 | | .562 | | | |
| | P2R2 vs. P2R3 | | .554 | | | |

## Table 5.2. Correlational estimates of reliabilities of single essays read by single readers (Sample A)

| Correlation | Reliability estimate | Average reliability within mode |
|---|---|---|
| *Narrative essays* | | .366 |
| N1R1 vs. N2R2 | .436 | |
| N1R1 vs. N2R3 | .239 | |
| N1R2 vs. N2R1 | .464 | |
| N1R2 vs. N2R3 | .230 | |
| N1R3 vs. N2R1 | .364 | |
| N1R3 vs. N2R2 | .466 | |
| *Expository essays* | | .400 |
| E1R1 vs. E2R2 | .358 | |
| E1R1 vs. E2R3 | .488 | |
| E1R2 vs. E2R1 | .357 | |
| E1R2 vs. E2R3 | .412 | |
| E1R3 vs. E2R1 | .386 | |
| E1R3 vs. E2R2 | .401 | |
| *Persuasive essays* | | .474 |
| P1R1 vs. P2R2 | .490 | |
| P1R1 vs. P2R3 | .414 | |
| P1R2 vs. P2R1 | .533 | |
| P1R2 vs. P2R3 | .438 | |
| P1R3 vs. P2R1 | .486 | |
| P1R3 vs. P2R2 | .481 | |

# Analysis of variance estimates of reliability

A more accurate procedure for making reliability estimates is the analysis of variance. In this procedure a model is formulated to explain variation in scores as determined by the various sources of error present. The following model was formulated to represent the sources of error in the essay assessment of this study:

$$Y_{emtr} = \mu + \alpha_e + \beta_m + \tau_{t(m)} + \rho_{r(m)} + \alpha\beta_{em} + \alpha\tau_{et(m)} + \alpha\rho_{er(m)} + \tau\rho_{tr(m)} + \epsilon_{emtr}$$

where

$Y_{emtr}$ = response of examinee $e$ to topic $t$ in mode $m$ when read by reader $r$

$\mu$ = mean response across all examinees

$\alpha_e$ = random variation associated with examinee $e$

$\beta_m$ = fixed deviation associated with mode of discourse $m$

$\tau_{t(m)}$ = random variation associated with topic $t$ (within mode $m$)

$\rho_{r(m)}$ = random variation associated with reader $r$ (within mode $m$)

$\alpha\beta_{em}$ = random variation associated with examinee by mode interaction

$\alpha\tau_{et(m)}$ = random variation associated with examinee by topic interaction (within mode)

$\alpha\rho_{er(m)}$ = random variation associated with examinee by reader interaction (within mode)

$\tau\rho_{tr(m)}$ = random variation associated with topic by reader interaction (within mode)

$\epsilon_{emtr}$ = variation unexplained, or error

From the above model, variance components can be developed for each of the sources of variation, and reliability estimates can be computed.

Estimates of reliabilities of observed total scores over all three modes, two topics per mode and three readers per mode, of this investigation were made as follows:

$$r_{xx} = \cfrac{\sigma_\alpha^2 + \cfrac{\sigma_{\alpha\beta}^2}{M}}{\sigma_\alpha^2 + \cfrac{\sigma_{\alpha\beta}^2}{M} + \cfrac{\sigma_\tau^2 + \sigma_{\alpha\tau}^2}{MT} + \cfrac{\sigma_\rho^2 + \sigma_{\alpha\rho}^2}{MR} + \cfrac{\sigma_{\tau\rho}^2 + \sigma_\epsilon^2}{MTR}}$$

where

$\sigma^2$ values = variances associated with various sources of error

$M$ = number of modes

$T$ = number of topics per mode

$R$ = number of readers per mode

The reliability of the observed mean score over all readings of the six essays was estimated at .876 using the above relationship. This reliability is, under the model, the expected correlation between the total (or mean) score obtained in the current experiment and the score that would be obtained if the experiment were rerun with the *same* three modes, two *new* topics within each mode, and three *new* readers within each mode, where each reader reads both topics within a mode. The same relationship can be used to estimate reliabilities over all three modes for different numbers of topics and readers.

Under an analogous model, but without the mode effect, the reliability of the obtained total within-mode score (that is, for the total score for two topics within mode each read by the same three readers) is

$$r_{mm} = \frac{\sigma_\alpha^2}{\sigma_\alpha^2 + \dfrac{\sigma_\tau^2 + \sigma_{\alpha\tau}^2}{T} + \dfrac{\sigma_\rho^2 + \sigma_{\alpha\rho}^2}{R} + \dfrac{\sigma_{\tau\rho}^2 + \sigma_\epsilon^2}{TR}}$$

Table 5.3 contains estimates of reliabilities within mode, and for all three modes combined, developed from the above relationships. The within-mode estimates for single readers are not substantially different from the correlational estimates of Table 5.2 (shown in parentheses). But estimates stepped up by using the Spearman-Brown formula are considerably higher than the analysis of variance estimates.

Reliabilities were also estimated for Sample D. For the total of all readings in all modes, an estimate of .899 was obtained. The mode reliabilities were .730 (narrative), .750 (expository), and .802 (persuasive).

The analysis-of-variance model was used, finally, to estimate reliabilities for hypothetical essay assessments in which each reader reads only one topic. For this hypothetical situation, the reliabilities would be estimated as

$$r_{hh} = \frac{\sigma_\alpha^2 + \dfrac{\sigma_{\alpha\beta}^2}{M}}{\sigma_\alpha^2 + \dfrac{\sigma_{\alpha\beta}^2}{M} + \dfrac{\sigma_\tau^2 + \sigma_{\alpha\tau}^2}{MT} + \dfrac{\sigma_\rho^2 + \sigma_{\alpha\rho}^2 + \sigma_{\tau\rho}^2 + \sigma_\epsilon^2}{MTR}}$$

Over all modes, topics, and readers, this relationship yields an estimate of .881, which is only slightly higher than the .876 figure obtained for observed scores (as obtained in this investigation). Table 5.4 shows reliabilities that would be expected under this hypothetical situation for a variety of assessments.

Table 5.4 can be used to approximate what reliabilities might be expected with different types of essay assessments. Specific essay types—narrative, expository, persuasive—are ignored in this analysis, but numbers of essays, modes, and readers per essay are considered. A single essay with one reading would be expected to yield a low reliability (.42). Adding a second reading, but still using only one essay, would increase reliability some (to .53). Using two topics in different discourse modes, with each being read by two different readers, would yield a slightly higher reliability (.57). Three essays, all of different discourse modes and each read by three readers, yields a much higher reliability (.79). To achieve reliability levels similar to those of standardized multiple-choice tests (.85–.95) would require at least four essays and at least two modes of discourse. For example, a reliability of .85 is estimated for an assessment using nine essays, three modes, and one reading per essay. Alternatively, a reliability of .86 is estimated for six essays, two modes, and two readings of each essay. Obviously, much effort is required to achieve high reliabilities with all-essay assessments.

Analysis-of-variance tables for the analyses de-

### Table 5.3. Analysis of variance reliability estimates for different combinations of modes, topics, and readers (Sample A)

| | Number of readers per topic | | |
|---|---|---|---|
| Topics per mode | 1 | 2 | 3 |
| *Narrative mode* | | | |
| 1 | .356 (.366)[a] | .472 (.536)[b] | .529 (.634)[b] |
| 2 | .507 | .627 | .681 |
| *Expository mode* | | | |
| 1 | .395 (.400) | .493 (.571)[b] | .538 (.667)[b] |
| 2 | .536 | .640 | .684 |
| *Persuasive mode* | | | |
| 1 | .463 (.474) | .574 (.643)[b] | .624 (.730)[b] |
| 2 | .534 | .720 | .761 |
| *All modes* | | | |
| 1 | .660 | .752 | .836 |
| 2 | .645 | .850 | .876 |

a. Correlational estimates from Table 5.2 are given in parentheses for comparison.
b. Spearman-Brown formula estimates, based on correlational estimates, are given in parentheses for comparison.

### Table 5.4. Estimated reliabilities for hypothetical essay examinations (Sample A)

| Number of modes | Number of topics per mode | Total essays | Number of readers per essay | | | | |
|---|---|---|---|---|---|---|---|
| | | | 1 | 2 | 3 | 4 | ∞ |
| 1 | 1 | 1 | .42 | .53 | .58 | .63 | .72 |
| | 2 | 2 | .59 | .70 | .74 | .77 | .84 |
| | 3 | 3 | .69 | .77 | .81 | .84 | .89 |
| 2 | 1 | 2 | .57 | .68 | .72 | .76 | .83 |
| | 2 | 4 | .73 | .81 | .84 | .86 | .90 |
| | 3 | 6 | .80 | .86 | .88 | .90 | .93 |
| 3 | 1 | 3 | .66 | .75 | .79 | .82 | .87 |
| | 2 | 6 | .80 | .86 | .88 | .90 | .93 |
| | 3 | 9 | .85 | .90 | .92 | .93 | .95 |

scribed are in Appendix F, Tables F.23 through F.30.

## Reliabilities of error counts

To control costs for the error counts, these were limited to the 94 cases of Sample D, and not all readers read all essays within mode. Rather, readers were randomly assigned so that each essay was subjected to two readings. The error counts from the two readings were then averaged. The correlations between the error counts were stepped up by the Spearman-Brown formula to obtain estimates of the reliabilities of the averaged error counts (Table 5.5). Counts of spelling errors yielded the highest reliabilities (.96).

### Table 5.5. Reliabilities of error counts (Sample D)

| Error type | Interreading correlation | Estimated reliability |
|---|---|---|
| Grammar | .6956 | .82 |
| Usage/diction | .7090 | .83 |
| Sentence structure | .6801 | .81 |
| GUSS errors[a] | .8765 | .93 |
| Punctuation | .6059 | .75 |
| Spelling | .9309 | .96 |
| Capitalization, etc. | .5794 | .73 |
| PSC errors | .8287 | .91 |
| Total errors | .8980 | .95 |

a. Estimates were also made of GUSS error counts within mode:

| Mode | GUSS reliability |
|---|---|
| Narrative | .81 |
| Expository | .91 |
| Persuasive | .80 |

## 6. Predictive validity analyses

We examined the predictive validity of both essay and non essay assessments of writing skill through the relationships between scores received from those assessments and three outcomes: actual writing performance on other essay assessments, instructors' judgments of students' writing skill, and grades assigned in a college freshman English composition course. The writing performance criterion consisted of the summation of scores on all essays other than the specific essay topic being evaluated. In other words, the writing performance criterion asks to what degree a given essay topic predicts performance on the remaining five topics. Instructors' judgments of writing ability represent the summation of two ratings made by instructors: student discourse skills and student mechanics skills. The course grade is simply the grade received by a student in the freshman English course in which the essays were written. Since both instructors' ratings and course grades may have been influenced by the specific essay being evaluated, there exists the possibility of some artificial inflation of validities when these last two criteria are used.

## *Predictive validities of essay assessments*

Tables 6.1 through 6.4 present analyses of the validity of the essay assessments as they relate to the three criteria. The four tables represent analyses conducted for four different samples of data. The samples are important for subsequent analyses because the data available for each sample are slightly different. Table 6.1 shows the validities obtained when relationships were based on the total sample of 267 cases. As would be expected, the correlations between essay scores and criteria increase as the number of readings increases. These increases in correlational relationships result primarily from increases in reliabilities of the essay assessments. The correlations with the writing performance criterion suggest that the expository essays were the most effective as predictors of performance on the remaining essays. Since the readers had more experience scoring expository essays than they had with the other two types, higher correlations may be expected. The correlations with instructors' judgments of students' writing abilities and course grades indicate that the persuasive essays were the best predictors of these outcomes. More time and effort were expended in preparing the persuasive essays, and they were much longer

## Table 6.1. Predictive validities of essay assessments for total sample of 267 cases (Sample A)

| Essay type | Topic | Number of readings | Correlations with | | |
| --- | --- | --- | --- | --- | --- |
| | | | Writing performance | Instructors' judgments | Course grade |
| Narrative | "Family Traditions" | 1 | .51 | .39 | .37 |
| | | 2 | .58 | .43 | .42 |
| | | 3 | .62 | .46 | .44 |
| | "Significant Event" | 1 | .53 | .41 | .37 |
| | | 2 | .60 | .47 | .41 |
| | | 3 | .64 | .49 | .44 |
| Expository | "Status Symbols" | 1 | .57 | .35 | .32 |
| | | 2 | .64 | .39 | .36 |
| | | 3 | .67 | .41 | .38 |
| | "Cornerstone" | 1 | .57 | .41 | .37 |
| | | 2 | .64 | .46 | .42 |
| | | 3 | .67 | .48 | .44 |
| Persuasive | "Drinking and Driving" | 1 | .55 | .49 | .46 |
| | | 2 | .61 | .54 | .50 |
| | | 3 | .63 | .57 | .52 |
| | "Book Censorship" | 1 | .52 | .47 | .43 |
| | | 2 | .58 | .52 | .48 |
| | | 3 | .60 | .55 | .50 |

than the other two types; thus, they may be more representative of a student's writing skill. Comparisons of the different essay types are confounded by two factors, however: (1) Since readers were nested within essay type, observed differences for any particular essay type may be due merely to reader differences. (2) Since the persuasive essays were written last (and close to the time instructors' ratings and grades were assigned), they may have influenced instructors' judgments and course grades more than did other essay types.

Because the total sample of 267 cases represented in Table 6.1 did not have English Composition Test (ECT) scores for all cases and because ECT scores were essential for some analyses, three smaller samples of data were de-

veloped, each slightly different. Table 6.2 is based on a sample of 210 cases, all having ECT scores. Some of the ECT scores in this sample were derived from special administrations of the test, which required approximate score equating procedures. The results given in Table 6.2 are similar to those obtained for the larger sample.

Table 6.3 is based on a sample of 141 cases, all with ECT scores from regular administrations of the test. Some of the ECT scores in this sample contain essay components, but all ECT scores were developed using standard score equating procedures. The results in Table 6.3 are similar to those obtained with the larger samples in Tables 6.1 and 6.2.

Table 6.4 is based on a sample of 94 cases, all with ECT scores developed from non-essay as-

## Table 6.2. Predictive validities of essay assessments for sample of 210 cases with ECT scores (Sample B)

| Essay type | Topic | Number of readings | Writing performance | Instructors' judgments | Course grade |
|---|---|---|---|---|---|
| | | | Correlations with | | |
| Narrative | "Family Traditions" | 1 | .52 | .38 | .40 |
| | | 2 | .59 | .43 | .44 |
| | | 3 | .62 | .45 | .46 |
| | "Significant Event" | 1 | .52 | .40 | .39 |
| | | 2 | .59 | .46 | .45 |
| | | 3 | .62 | .48 | .47 |
| Expository | "Status Symbols" | 1 | .59 | .38 | .37 |
| | | 2 | .66 | .42 | .42 |
| | | 3 | .69 | .44 | .43 |
| | "Cornerstone" | 1 | .59 | .45 | .43 |
| | | 2 | .66 | .50 | .48 |
| | | 3 | .69 | .53 | .50 |
| Persuasive | "Drinking and Driving" | 1 | .56 | .50 | .48 |
| | | 2 | .61 | .55 | .53 |
| | | 3 | .63 | .57 | .55 |
| | "Book Censorship" | 1 | .53 | .45 | .41 |
| | | 2 | .59 | .50 | .46 |
| | | 3 | .61 | .52 | .48 |

sessments. The results are generally similar to those obtained with the larger samples, but the persuasive essays do not stand out as correlating highest with instructors' judgments and course grades as they do in the other samples. Perhaps the confoundings noted above were operating less in this sample than in the other samples.

## Predictive validities of non-essay assessments

Table 6.5 gives the correlations between non-essay assessments and the same three criteria used in Tables 6.1 through 6.4. Note that the writing performance criterion is different in this table, depending on which of the six essays was removed (indicated by the abbreviations WP1, WP2, WP3, WP4, WP5, and WP6). The abbreviation WP1, for example, indicates that the first narrative essay was removed.

Comparisons of the non-essay assessments may be made with the essay assessments within samples. Multiple correlations of non-essay assessments—combining Scholastic Aptitude Test (SAT)-verbal, Test of Standard Written English (TSWE), and English Composition Test (ECT)—show that they are clearly better predictors of the writing performance criterion than are single essays with one reading. Non-essay assessments are roughly equivalent to single-essay assessments with two readings. Some essays (persuasive) appear to be better predictors of instructors' judgments. In all of these comparisons, however, it should be kept in mind that more time and

*Table 6.3. Predictive validities of essay assessments for sample of 141 cases with ECT scores (Sample C)*

| Essay type | Topic | Number of readings | Correlations with | | |
| --- | --- | --- | --- | --- | --- |
| | | | Writing performance | Instructors' judgments | Course grade |
| Narrative | "Family Traditions" | 1 | .58 | .39 | .40 |
| | | 2 | .66 | .44 | .45 |
| | | 3 | .70 | .46 | .47 |
| | "Significant Event" | 1 | .52 | .42 | .42 |
| | | 2 | .59 | .47 | .48 |
| | | 3 | .62 | .49 | .50 |
| Expository | "Status Symbols" | 1 | .60 | .35 | .39 |
| | | 2 | .67 | .40 | .43 |
| | | 3 | .70 | .42 | .46 |
| | "Cornerstone" | 1 | .60 | .40 | .42 |
| | | 2 | .67 | .44 | .47 |
| | | 3 | .70 | .46 | .49 |
| Persuasive | "Drinking and Driving" | 1 | .53 | .46 | .45 |
| | | 2 | .59 | .51 | .50 |
| | | 3 | .61 | .53 | .52 |
| | "Book Censorship" | 1 | .54 | .47 | .44 |
| | | 2 | .61 | .53 | .50 |
| | | 3 | .65 | .57 | .53 |

greater effort are required to produce the essay scores (especially the persuasive essay scores) than to produce the non-essay scores.

In Table 6.5, Sample D tended to yield higher correlations than did Samples A, B, or C. When all six essays were used for the criterion, the correlation with the TSWE, for example, was .71 in Sample D and .63 in Sample A. Much, but not all, of this difference was removed by a correction for restriction of range. Corrected correlations were .78 in Sample D and .74 in Sample A. (See Appendix E, note 7.)

## Predictive validities of assessment combinations

Table 6.6 shows the predictive correlations obtained when essay and non-essay assessments are used in combination. For these analyses the TSWE, the ECT, and one essay were used to predict the three criteria. Only two of the samples were used (B and D) because ECT scores were not available for all cases in Sample A and because Sample C includes some ECT scores based in part on essays. In Sample B the essay components have been removed from ECT scores statistically. Sample B also includes ECT scores developed from special administrations where equating with other ECT scores was only approximate. Sample D, while smaller, contains ECT scores that are theoretically optimum for these analyses because they contain no essay component and because all equating was conducted as a part of routine test administration procedures.

An observation can be made from Table 6.6 that when essay assessments are used in combi-

*Table 6.4. Predictive validities of essay assessments for sample of 94 cases with all-multiple-choice ECT scores (Sample D)*

| Essay type | Topic | Number of readings | Correlations with | | |
| --- | --- | --- | --- | --- | --- |
| | | | Writing performance | Instructors' judgments | Course grade |
| Narrative | "Family Traditions" | 1 | .59 | .37 | .42 |
| | | 2 | .66 | .42 | .47 |
| | | 3 | .69 | .44 | .49 |
| | "Significant Event" | 1 | .54 | .41 | .46 |
| | | 2 | .60 | .46 | .52 |
| | | 3 | .63 | .48 | .55 |
| Expository | "Status Symbols" | 1 | .65 | .39 | .47 |
| | | 2 | .72 | .44 | .51 |
| | | 3 | .75 | .45 | .53 |
| | "Cornerstone" | 1 | .59 | .38 | .42 |
| | | 2 | .68 | .43 | .48 |
| | | 3 | .71 | .45 | .50 |
| Persuasive | "Drinking and Driving" | 1 | .56 | .41 | .43 |
| | | 2 | .62 | .46 | .47 |
| | | 3 | .64 | .47 | .49 |
| | "Book Censorship" | 1 | .50 | .37 | .37 |
| | | 2 | .59 | .44 | .43 |
| | | 3 | .64 | .48 | .47 |

nation with non-essay assessments, the number of readings of the essay is relatively less important than it is otherwise. In most cases there is not a great deal of difference between the correlations for one reading and those for three readings.

A second observation is that there is not much difference among the essay topics or discourse modes. The first expository essay ("Status Symbols") yielded the highest correlations with the writing performance criterion. But the first persuasive essay ("Drinking and Driving") yielded the best correlations with instructors' judgments of writing ability and course grades in Sample B, and the second narrative essay ("Significant Event") yielded the best correlations with the same criteria in Sample D. Averaging over all criteria and both samples results in a slight ad-

vantage for "Drinking and Driving" (average $R = .65$). "Family Traditions" is the only essay topic with an average multiple correlation of less than .60 when three readings were used.

## Incremental predictive validities of essay assessments

Table 6.7 shows predictive validity increments for essay assessments beyond what is possible using non-essay assessments (TSWE and ECT) alone. These differences represent the contribution of the essay to the prediction of the outcomes of interest. This analysis makes it clear that essay assessments can contribute substantially to the prediction of important outcomes. The average increments over all criteria and samples suggest

## Table 6.5. Predictive validities of non-essay assessments

| Sample | Predictor(s) | Correlations with | | | | | | | Instructors' judgments | Course grade |
|--------|--------------|------|------|------|------|------|------|------|-----------|------------|
| | | WP0[a] | WP1[b] | WP2[c] | WP3[d] | WP4[e] | WP5[f] | WP6[g] | | |
| A (N = 267) | SAT-V | .55 | .52 | .55 | .53 | .54 | .55 | .55 | .46 | .44 |
| | TSWE | .63 | .59 | .62 | .62 | .63 | .62 | .64 | .48 | .41 |
| | SAT-V and TSWE | | .61 | .64 | .63 | .65 | .64 | .65 | .51 | .46 |
| B (N = 210) | SAT-V | .54 | .51 | .54 | .53 | .53 | .53 | .55 | .47 | .48 |
| | TSWE | .63 | .60 | .63 | .61 | .63 | .62 | .64 | .49 | .45 |
| | ECT | .61 | .58 | .62 | .61 | .61 | .58 | .61 | .50 | .44 |
| | SAT-V and TSWE | | .62 | .65 | .63 | .64 | .63 | .66 | .52 | .51 |
| | SAT-V and ECT | | .60 | .64 | .63 | .63 | .61 | .64 | .53 | .51 |
| | TSWE and ECT | | .62 | .66 | .65 | .65 | .63 | .66 | .52 | .47 |
| C (N = 141) | SAT-V | .54 | .49 | .54 | .52 | .53 | .55 | .54 | .36 | .37 |
| | TSWE | .69 | .64 | .69 | .68 | .69 | .69 | .69 | .45 | .42 |
| | ECT | .62 | .58 | .63 | .62 | .62 | .63 | .62 | .47 | .41 |
| | SAT-V and TSWE | | .65 | .69 | .68 | .69 | .70 | .70 | .46 | .44 |
| | SAT-V and ECT | | .59 | .64 | .63 | .64 | .65 | .64 | .47 | .42 |
| | TSWE and ECT | | .65 | .69 | .69 | .69 | .70 | .69 | .48 | .43 |
| D (N = 94) | SAT-V | .57 | .52 | .57 | .56 | .56 | .59 | .59 | .42 | .42 |
| | TSWE | .71 | .66 | .70 | .71 | .71 | .72 | .71 | .47 | .45 |
| | ECT | .66 | .62 | .66 | .67 | .66 | .66 | .66 | .52 | .44 |
| | SAT-V and TSWE | | .66 | .71 | .71 | .71 | .73 | .72 | .49 | .47 |
| | SAT-V and ECT | | .62 | .67 | .68 | .67 | .68 | .68 | .52 | .46 |
| | TSWE and ECT | | .66 | .71 | .71 | .71 | .73 | .72 | .52 | .46 |

*Note:* WP = writing performance.
a. WP0 = summation of all six essay scores (all 18 ratings).
b. WP1 = summation of five essays with "Family Traditions" removed.
c. WP2 = summation of five essays with "Significant Event" removed.
d. WP3 = summation of five essays with "Status Symbols" removed.
e. WP4 = summation of five essays with "Cornerstone" removed.
f. WP5 = summation of five essays with "Drinking and Driving" removed.
g. WP6 = summation of five essays with "Book Censorship" removed.

a slight preference for the first persuasive essay ("Drinking and Driving"), although all other topics except the first narrative essay were close seconds.

## Incremental predictive validities of multiple-choice tests

Table 6.8 shows predictive validity increments for the TSWE beyond what was possible using the essay assessments alone. Again, three criteria and two samples were used for the analyses. Here one observes that the average increment over all samples and criteria *decreases* as the number of essay readings is increased. This result shows, as might be expected, that the multiple-choice test contributes most when the essay assessment is conducted with the fewest independent scorings. But the contribution was still substantial when up to three readings of each essay were conducted. As a multiple-choice test twice as long as the TSWE, the ECT might reasonably be expected

## Table 6.6. Predictive validities of assessments combining essay and non-essay components

| Essay assessment | Number of readings | Sample B ($N = 210$): Multiple correlations ($R$) with | | | Sample D ($N = 94$): Multiple correlations ($R$) with | | | Average $R$ |
|---|---|---|---|---|---|---|---|---|
| | | Writing performance | Instructors' judgments | Course grade | Writing performance | Instructors' judgments | Course grade | |
| "Family Traditions" | 1 | .67 | .54 | .51 | .70 | .53 | .49 | .57 |
| | 2 | .69 | .55 | .52 | .72 | .53 | .51 | .59 |
| | 3 | .70 | .55 | .52 | .73 | .53 | .52 | .59 |
| "Significant Event" | 1 | .73 | .57 | .53 | .75 | .57 | .55 | .62 |
| | 2 | .75 | .59 | .55 | .76 | .58 | .57 | .63 |
| | 3 | .76 | .60 | .56 | .77 | .59 | .59 | .64 |
| "Status Symbols" | 1 | .73 | .55 | .50 | .79 | .56 | .54 | .61 |
| | 2 | .75 | .56 | .51 | .82 | .56 | .56 | .63 |
| | 3 | .77 | .56 | .52 | .83 | .56 | .57 | .64 |
| "Cornerstone" | 1 | .73 | .58 | .53 | .77 | .55 | .52 | .61 |
| | 2 | .76 | .60 | .55 | .80 | .56 | .54 | .64 |
| | 3 | .77 | .61 | .56 | .81 | .56 | .55 | .64 |
| "Drinking and Driving" | 1 | .70 | .60 | .56 | .78 | .57 | .53 | .62 |
| | 2 | .72 | .62 | .58 | .80 | .58 | .55 | .64 |
| | 3 | .73 | .63 | .59 | .80 | .58 | .55 | .65 |
| "Book Censorship" | 1 | .73 | .59 | .54 | .76 | .56 | .51 | .62 |
| | 2 | .75 | .61 | .56 | .78 | .57 | .53 | .63 |
| | 3 | .76 | .62 | .56 | .79 | .58 | .54 | .64 |

*Note:* TSWE and ECT scores (non-essay assessments), were used in combination with the indicated essay to predict the three criteria.

to have greater incremental validity. Table 6.9 shows this to be the case, though the increments for the ECT are not a great deal more than those for the TSWE. While the SAT-verbal test is not a test of writing skill per se, it does tap verbal skills important in writing. Table 6.10 shows that the SAT-verbal score has incremental predictive validity of the same order of magnitude as that of TSWE and ECT.

A comparison of these three multiple-choice tests in terms of the average increment over all six writing sample scores gives a slight edge to the ECT with an overall average increment of .08. The SAT-verbal score had an overall average increment of .07 and the TSWE, .06.

## Table 6.7. *Incremental predictive validities of essay assessments*

| Topic | Number of readings | Writing performance | | Instructors' judgments | | Course grade | | Average increment |
|---|---|---|---|---|---|---|---|---|
| | | Sample B | Sample D | Sample B | Sample D | Sample B | Sample D | |
| "Family | 1 | .05 | .04 | .02 | .01 | .04 | .01 | .03 |
| Traditions" | 2 | .07 | .06 | .03 | .01 | .05 | .01 | .04 |
| | 3 | .08 | .07 | .03 | .01 | .05 | .01 | .05 |
| "Significant | 1 | .07 | .04 | .05 | .05 | .06 | .05 | .06 |
| Event" | 2 | .09 | .05 | .07 | .06 | .07 | .06 | .07 |
| | 3 | .10 | .06 | .08 | .07 | .09 | .07 | .08 |
| "Status | 1 | .08 | .08 | .02 | .04 | .03 | .04 | .06 |
| Symbols" | 2 | .10 | .11 | .04 | .04 | .04 | .04 | .07 |
| | 3 | .12 | .12 | .04 | .04 | .05 | .04 | .08 |
| "Cornerstone" | 1 | .08 | .06 | .06 | .03 | .06 | .03 | .06 |
| | 2 | .11 | .08 | .08 | .04 | .07 | .04 | .06 |
| | 3 | .12 | .10 | .09 | .04 | .09 | .04 | .08 |
| "Drinking | 1 | .07 | .05 | .09 | .05 | .09 | .05 | .07 |
| and Driving" | 2 | .09 | .07 | .10 | .06 | .11 | .06 | .08 |
| | 3 | .10 | .07 | .11 | .06 | .12 | .06 | .09 |
| "Book | 1 | .07 | .04 | .07 | .04 | .07 | .04 | .06 |
| Censorship" | 2 | .09 | .06 | .09 | .05 | .09 | .05 | .07 |
| | 3 | .10 | .07 | .10 | .06 | .09 | .06 | .08 |

*Note*: The increment is the difference in multiple correlations between using TSWE, ECT, and the essay and using only TSWE and ECT. Where more than a single reading is involved, reported figures are averages.

## Table 6.8. Incremental predictive validity of TSWE

| Topic | Number of readings | Writing performance | | Instructors' judgments | | Course grade | | Average increment |
|---|---|---|---|---|---|---|---|---|
| | | Sample B | Sample D | Sample B | Sample D | Sample B | Sample D | |
| "Family | 1 | .14 | .09 | .14 | .11 | .10 | .06 | .11 |
| Traditions" | 2 | .09 | .05 | .10 | .06 | .07 | .03 | .07 |
| | 3 | .07 | .04 | .08 | .04 | .05 | .02 | .05 |
| "Significant | 1 | .19 | .10 | .15 | .12 | .12 | .08 | .13 |
| Event" | 2 | .14 | .07 | .10 | .08 | .08 | .04 | .08 |
| | 3 | .12 | .05 | .09 | .07 | .07 | .03 | .07 |
| "Status | 1 | .12 | .14 | .14 | .12 | .11 | .06 | .12 |
| Symbols" | 2 | .08 | .09 | .11 | .08 | .08 | .04 | .08 |
| | 3 | .06 | .08 | .09 | .07 | .07 | .01 | .06 |
| "Cornerstone" | 1 | .13 | .10 | .11 | .13 | .09 | .09 | .11 |
| | 2 | .09 | .08 | .08 | .09 | .06 | .05 | .08 |
| | 3 | .08 | .06 | .06 | .08 | .05 | .00 | .06 |
| "Drinking | 1 | .14 | .09 | .09 | .13 | .07 | 10 | .10 |
| and Driving" | 2 | .11 | .06 | .06 | .09 | .04 | .07 | .07 |
| | 3 | .09 | .05 | .04 | .09 | .03 | .04 | .06 |
| "Book | 1 | .19 | .08 | .12 | .15 | .12 | .13 | .13 |
| Censorship" | 2 | .15 | .05 | .09 | .10 | .09 | .09 | .09 |
| | 3 | .14 | .03 | .09 | .07 | .08 | .03 | .07 |

*Note*: Incremental predictive validity is defined as the multiple correlation of TSWE and an essay score (for predicting the criterion) *minus* the correlation between the same essay score and the same criterion.

## Table 6.9. Incremental predictive validity of ECT

| Topic | Number of readings | Writing performance | | Instructors' judgments | | Course grade | | Average increment |
|---|---|---|---|---|---|---|---|---|
| | | Sample B | Sample D | Sample B | Sample D | Sample B | Sample D | |
| "Family | 1 | .12 | .09 | .15 | .16 | .10 | .07 | .12 |
| Traditions" | 2 | .08 | .05 | .11 | .11 | .07 | .04 | .08 |
| | 3 | .06 | .03 | .10 | .09 | .06 | .03 | .06 |
| "Significant | 1 | .19 | .18 | .17 | .16 | .13 | .08 | .15 |
| Event" | 2 | .16 | .14 | .12 | .12 | .09 | .07 | .12 |
| | 3 | .13 | .12 | .11 | .11 | .08 | .04 | .10 |
| "Status | 1 | .13 | .13 | .16 | .17 | .12 | .07 | .13 |
| Symbols" | 2 | .11 | .09 | .13 | .12 | .09 | .05 | .10 |
| | 3 | .07 | .07 | .12 | .11 | .08 | .04 | .08 |
| "Cornerstone" | 1 | .12 | .15 | .12 | .17 | .09 | .09 | .12 |
| | 2 | .09 | .09 | .09 | .13 | .07 | .06 | .09 |
| | 3 | .07 | .08 | .07 | .11 | .06 | .09 | .08 |
| "Drinking | 1 | .11 | .18 | .09 | .16 | .07 | .07 | .11 |
| and Driving" | 2 | .08 | .14 | .06 | .12 | .04 | .06 | .08 |
| | 3 | .07 | .12 | .04 | .11 | .03 | .13 | .08 |
| "Book | 1 | .17 | .22 | .13 | .19 | .11 | .15 | .16 |
| Censorship" | 2 | .13 | .16 | .10 | .13 | .09 | .09 | .12 |
| | 3 | .12 | .12 | .09 | .10 | .08 | .06 | .10 |

*Note*: Incremental predictive validity is defined as the multiple correlation of ECT and an essay score (for predicting the criterion) *minus* the correlation between the same essay score and the same criterion.

## Table 6.10. Incremental predictive validity of SAT-verbal score

| Topic | Number of readings | Writing performance | | Instructors' judgments | | Course grade | | Average increment |
|---|---|---|---|---|---|---|---|---|
| | | Sample B | Sample D | Sample B | Sample D | Sample B | Sample D | |
| "Family | 1 | .10 | .05 | .14 | .09 | .13 | .06 | .10 |
| Traditions" | 2 | .06 | .02 | .10 | .05 | .10 | .03 | .06 |
| | 3 | .05 | .01 | .09 | .04 | .09 | .02 | .05 |
| "Significant | 1 | .14 | .12 | .15 | .10 | .16 | .08 | .12 |
| Event" | 2 | .10 | .10 | .11 | .07 | .12 | .05 | .09 |
| | 3 | .09 | .08 | .10 | .06 | .11 | .03 | .08 |
| "Status | 1 | .08 | .07 | .14 | .09 | .15 | .05 | .10 |
| Symbols" | 2 | .05 | .04 | .11 | .06 | .12 | .04 | .07 |
| | 3 | .04 | .03 | .10 | .05 | .11 | .03 | .06 |
| "Cornerstone" | 1 | .09 | .10 | .10 | .10 | .12 | .08 | .10 |
| | 2 | .06 | .05 | .08 | .07 | .09 | .05 | .07 |
| | 3 | .05 | .04 | .06 | .06 | .08 | .04 | .06 |
| "Drinking | 1 | .10 | .16 | .09 | .11 | .11 | .10 | .11 |
| and Driving" | 2 | .08 | .13 | .07 | .08 | .08 | .08 | .09 |
| | 3 | .07 | .12 | .05 | .08 | .07 | .07 | .08 |
| "Book | 1 | .14 | .19 | .12 | .13 | .15 | .13 | .14 |
| Censorship" | 2 | .11 | .14 | .09 | .09 | .12 | .10 | .11 |
| | 3 | .10 | .11 | .09 | .07 | .11 | .07 | .09 |

*Note*: Incremental predictive validity is defined as the multiple correlation of SAT-V and an essay score (for predicting the criterion) *minus* the correlation between the same essay score and the same criterion.

# 7. Construct validity analyses

The purpose of the analyses of this chapter is to provide a better understanding of what the essay scores measure and how that differs from what is measured by multiple-choice tests of writing skills. The ongoing dialogue between supporters of "objective" tests and supporters of essays as the more valid measures of writing ability will be more informative if empirical results can be brought to bear on the following questions:

- Is writing ability a single, generalizable construct, or is it likely to be rater-, content-, or mode-specific? That is, do judgments about a student's writing ability vary according to the rater, the topic assigned, or the requested mode of expression as opposed to some other mode? Is it possible that Jane is judged to be a very good writer when she writes in the narrative mode but a mediocre writer in the expository mode?
- If writing skill can be reasonably approximated by a single underlying factor model, is there one particular writing mode that appears to be the best measure of this overall writing ability?
- Does the empirical evidence based on essay data favor a single-factor or a multifactor model of judged writing ability? What is the relationship of this factor or these factors to multiple-choice test measures of writing ability?

We have attempted to shed additional light on the above questions by applying confirmatory factor analysis methods to essay rating data and then extending multiple-choice test measures into the factor space defined by the essay factors. The latter analysis (that is, the factor extension) attempted to describe the relationship between the multiple-choice measures of writing ability and the essay factor or factors.

## Sample and method

Sample A (267 cases) was used for these analyses. As described in Chapter 2, each student wrote essays on two topics within each of three discourse modes, and each essay was scored independently by three raters on a scale of 1 to 6 (see Table 2.1 for the overall experimental design).

Maximum likelihood estimation of the factor models was carried out using the LISREL6 program (Joreskog and Sorbom 1985). An orderly series of factor models were posed and tested. These started with the simplest model of writing ability—a single-factor model—and then tested progressively more complicated models.

The next, more complex model tested hypothesized a model of writing ability in which the students' performance on each of the three discursive modes could be assumed to reflect related but conceptually different writing skills. If the data were consistent with such a model, we might conclude that the mode factors had discriminant validity. An alternative factor model that was also tested included topics within modes as factors. If a model based on topic factors provided a good fit to the data, the presence of separate topic factors within modes suggests potential problems in the interpretation of essay grades. For example, if the rankings for topics A and B under the discourse mode are minimally correlated, how can we be sure that we are measuring a valid construct called discourse if its measurement varies by the topic given?

A hierarchical factor solution was also posed and tested. This model assumed a general writing ability factor (second-order factor) and six topic within-mode factors (first-order factors). This model addressed the question of which discursive mode is the best measure of general writing ability as defined by the single second-order factor. As used here, the term *best* refers to that mode or topic factor that shows the strongest correlation with the general writing ability factor. Maximum likelihood estimates of interrater reliabilities were also estimated from the various factor models in order to identify those topics or modes that seemed more prone to lead to disagreement among the raters.

Finally, factor extensions were carried out to examine the relationship between the multiple-choice measures of writing ability and the essay factors. In addition to casting further light on how the two measurement approaches may differ, this analysis attempted to gather external evidence with respect to the potential discriminant validity of the factors underlying the essay scores.

## Results

Table 7.1 presents the factor loadings and goodness-of-fit measures when the simplest of all models—the single-factor model—was fitted to the data. Inspection of the factor loadings along with the various goodness-of-fit measures suggests that while there is a substantial general factor, there remains sufficient unexplained common variance to support the further investigation of

*Table 7.1. Maximum likelihood estimates of factor loadings assuming single-factor model*

| Variables/readers | Loadings |
| --- | --- |
| Narrative 1, R1 | .534 |
| Narrative 1, R2 | .669 |
| Narrative 1, R3 | .552 |
| Narrative 2, R1 | .610 |
| Narrative 2, R2 | .674 |
| Narrative 2, R3 | .522 |
| Expository 1, R1 | .681 |
| Expository 1, R2 | .622 |
| Expository 1, R3 | .687 |
| Expository 2, R1 | .647 |
| Expository 2, R2 | .611 |
| Expository 2, R3 | .682 |
| Persuasive 1, R1 | .650 |
| Persuasive 1, R2 | .671 |
| Persuasive 1, R3 | .597 |
| Persuasive 2, R1 | .623 |
| Persuasive 2, R2 | .620 |
| Persuasive 2, R3 | .547 |

*Note*: GFI = .70; RMSR = .091; $X^2$ = 793.30; $df$ = 135; $p$ = 0.0; percentage of common variance = 78.14.

more complex models. Some of the goodness-of-fit measures computed in the LISREL6 program need additional explanation. The goodness-of-fit index (GFI) is a measure of the relative amount of variances and covariances that are jointly accounted for by the factor model. The index varies between 0 and 1; an index of 1 means that the factor model exactly reproduced the original correlation matrix.

The root mean square residual (RMSR) is a measure of the average absolute size of the residual correlations after the factor has been extracted. The $X^2$ goodness-of-fit measure along with its associated probability reflects the likelihood ratio test between the variance-covariance matrix conditional on the particular constrained factor model and an unconstrained version. The

$X^2$ probability reflects the probability of obtaining a larger $X^2$ given the observed variance-covariance matrix and given that the hypothesized factor model is correct. The $X^2$ statistic is strictly appropriate only for testing the hypothesis about variance-covariance matrices and not correlation matrices as used here; unlike the other two indices of goodness of fit, it is dependent on sample size. It is being reported here only to give one more rough measure of goodness of fit as we compare different factor models.

The GFI of .70 in Table 7.1 suggests a minimum fitting model, as does the RMSR of .091. A more familiar index of fit—the percentage of common variance—is also presented in Table 7.1. That is, approximately 78 percent of the common variance in the correlation matrix is explained by the single-factor model of writing ability. While the single-factor model does not fit all that well, the percentage of common variance explained along with the substantial factor loadings is certainly evidence that the between-individual variance across topics and modes is primarily explainable with a single general writing ability factor.

Inspection of the residual correlation matrix, however, indicates the presence of significant and systematic patterns of positive residuals among the raters within topics. To a much lesser extent, positive residuals were also present among the raters within mode. It was interesting to note that there was little or no correlated "error" for the same rater across topics within mode. The systematic patterns among the residuals along with the comparatively mediocre fit of the single-factor model argued for the fitting of both mode and topic factor models.

Table 7.2 presents the factor loadings, factor correlations, and goodness-of-fit indices for a constrained model based on three mode factors. All three goodness-of-fit indices suggest a relatively substantial improvement (over the baseline single-factor model) in the fit of the data to the hy-pothesized three-factor model based on mode of expression. Using the single-factor solution as a baseline, there is a 19 percent improvement in the GFI and a 36 percent improvement in the RMSR. The intercorrelations among the factors are relatively high, particularly between the narrative and the expository modes, while the persuasive mode factor is considerably more independent of the other two mode factors.

Although it is not substantial, there appears to be some discriminant validity for factors based on modes. It should be kept in mind that the factor intercorrelations are essentially correlations between hypothetical mode scores that have been corrected for attenuation. Given that frame of reference, one is less likely to infer that measures of the narrative and the expository modes are completely interchangeable. The fact remains, however, that most of the mode variance is due to differences between the persuasive mode factor and the other two.

The relatively low relationship between the persuasive mode factor and the other two mode factors is particularly interesting in light of the fact that essays written on the two topics in the persuasive mode were completed at home. Inspection of the size of the loadings for the raters on the persuasive factor suggests that there was greater agreement among raters when they reviewed essays in this mode than in the other two modes. This increased agreement is also accompanied by generally larger score variances in the persuasive mode. The question arises whether the increased variation in individual differences being recorded by the raters in this mode is a function of the type of writing or of uncontrolled influences.

Inspection of the residuals from the three-factor model suggests that additional improvement in fit may be arrived at if a model is fitted based on the six topic factors. Table 7.3 shows the factor loadings, intercorrelations, and goodness-of-fit indices for the six-factor topic model. The GFI

## Table 7.2. Maximum likelihood estimates of factor loadings assuming three mode factors

| Variables/readers | Factor 1 (Narrative) | Factor 2 (Expository) | Factor 3 (Persuasive) |
|---|---|---|---|
| Narrative 1, R1 | .626 | — | — |
| Narrative 1, R2 | .725 | — | — |
| Narrative 1, R3 | .623 | — | — |
| Narrative 2, R1 | .695 | — | — |
| Narrative 2, R2 | .769 | — | — |
| Narrative 2, R3 | .558 | — | — |
| Expository 1, R1 | — | .742 | — |
| Expository 1, R2 | — | .682 | — |
| Expository 1, R3 | — | .769 | — |
| Expository 2, R1 | — | .659 | — |
| Expository 2, R2 | — | .628 | — |
| Expository 2, R3 | — | .745 | — |
| Persuasive 1, R1 | — | — | .748 |
| Persuasive 1, R2 | — | — | .815 |
| Persuasive 1, R3 | — | — | .745 |
| Persuasive 2, R1 | — | — | .726 |
| Persuasive 2, R2 | — | — | .741 |
| Persuasive 2, R3 | — | — | .633 |
| *Factor intercorrelations* | | | |
| Factor 1 | 1.0 | | |
| Factor 2 | .815 | 1.0 | |
| Factor 3 | .612 | .654 | 1.0 |

*Note*: GFI = .831; RMSR =; .058; $X^2$ = 426.12; $df$ = 132.0; $p$ = 0.0.

showed a 32 percent improvement over the baseline single-factor solution. This equated to a 13 percent improvement beyond that of the three-factor mode model. There was a 43 percent improvement over the baseline model in the RMSR index and a considerable reduction in the $X^2$, suggesting considerable improvement over both the baseline and the three-factor model. Inspection of the residuals indicated that there were no systematic patterns of nonzero residuals left after fitting the six-topic-factor solution.

There are consistent increases in the factor loadings within each topic factor over those found in the baseline as well as in the mode-factor so-lution. The square of the factor loading can be interpreted as the reliability of a given rater within a given topic and mode. While the factor loadings showed consistent increases, the intercorrelations among the factors showed consistent decreases. The intercorrelations among the topic factors within mode (adjacent to the main diagonal) tend to be highest, as one would expect from the previous three-factor mode solution.

That the greatest improvement over the baseline single general factor model occurred when topic factors were fitted is not particularly good news. It appears that between-topic variance is at least as important in explaining individual dif-

## Table 7.3. *Maximum likelihood estimates of factor loadings assuming six topic factors*

| Variables/readers | Factor 1 | Factor 2 | Factor 3 | Factor 4 | Factor 5 | Factor 6 |
|---|---|---|---|---|---|---|
| Narrative 1, R1 | .709 | — | — | — | — | — |
| Narrative 1, R2 | .787 | — | — | — | — | — |
| Narrative 1, R3 | .659 | — | — | — | — | — |
| Narrative 2, R1 | — | .748 | — | — | — | — |
| Narrative 2, R2 | — | .794 | — | — | — | — |
| Narrative 2, R3 | — | .619 | — | — | — | — |
| Expository 1, R1 | — | — | .789 | — | — | — |
| Expository 1, R2 | — | — | .745 | — | — | — |
| Expository 1, R3 | — | — | .829 | — | — | — |
| Expository 2, R1 | — | — | — | .786 | — | — |
| Expository 2, R2 | — | — | — | .735 | — | — |
| Expository 2, R3 | — | — | — | .795 | — | — |
| Persuasive 1, R1 | — | — | — | — | .777 | — |
| Persuasive 1, R2 | — | — | — | — | .878 | — |
| Persuasive 1, R3 | — | — | — | — | .770 | — |
| Persuasive 2, R1 | — | — | — | — | — | .817 |
| Persuasive 2, R2 | — | — | — | — | — | .825 |
| Persuasive 2, R3 | — | — | — | — | — | .648 |

*Factor intercorrelations*

| | | | | | | |
|---|---|---|---|---|---|---|
| Factor 1 | 1.0 | | | | | |
| Factor 2 | .776 | 1.0 | | | | |
| Factor 3 | .678 | .772 | 1.0 | | | |
| Factor 4 | .651 | .629 | .698 | 1.0 | | |
| Factor 5 | .563 | .504 | .509 | .617 | 1.0 | |
| Factor 6 | .503 | .534 | .520 | .571 | .765 | 1.0 |

*Note*: GFI = .925; RMSR = .039; $X^2$ = 197.59; $df$ = 120.0; $p$ = 0.0.

ferences in essay performance as are variations in type of discursive mode. The relative importance of topic variance as compared with mode variance is roughly indicated by the following reliability analysis.

Table 7.4 presents maximum likelihood estimates of the reliabilities of the mean of three raters that would be expected if the ratings were done within topic and mode. The estimates are derived from the factor loading in the six-factor model. Where the factor model fits best, as in the six-factor solution, the factor model estimates are comparable with the correlational estimates given earlier in Table 5.1.

There appears to be a relatively large general writing ability factor, but it may be better to refer to this factor as a *standardized* writing ability factor because the majority of the writing measures were gathered in a standardized situation.

Table 7.5 presents the results of a hierarchical factor solution where the six topic factors are estimated as the first-order factors and a single standardized writing ability factor is simultaneously estimated as the second-order factor. Of interest here is the size of the loadings of the six first-order factors on the standardized factor. Inspection of Table 7.5 suggests that either the narrative mode or the expository mode will provide very good measurement of "general" writing ability as defined by the second-order factor. Both topic factors within the persuasive mode have lower loadings on this standardized factor. This finding is consistent with the earlier discussion with respect to the possibility that there may be other, uncontrolled sources of variation influencing students' performance on their essays in this mode. It is possible that the persuasive essays were measuring something different from what the narrative and the expository essays were measuring. It should also be kept in mind that the task as defined in the persuasive mode is closer to what is usually required in classroom writing assignments. That is, the writing task is often assigned as homework. Thus, in a sense, the assignment as outlined in the persuasive mode comes closest to a simulation of a normal classroom writing assignment.

## Factor extension

The analysis up to this point has been entirely internal. Table 7.6 shows the loadings of various objective test measures of writing ability, selected demographics, and other school performance measures on the factors fitted in the six-factor topic model. That is, Table 7.6 shows the results of extending the external measures on each of the six factors. The loadings of the extended variables may be interpreted as correlations among the six topic factors and the extended variables.

Of interest here is the overall level of the loadings as well as the possibility of differentiation in the pattern of loadings. The internal analysis argued for the discriminant validity of the mode factors. Additional external support for this position would take the form of differential loading patterns of the multiple-choice tests, the past

*Table 7.4. Reliabilities of mean of three raters based on factor analytic model*

| Topic | Reliability |
|---|---|
| Narrative 1 | .751 |
| Narrative 2 | .754 |
| Expository 1 | .834 |
| Expository 2 | .816 |
| Persuasive 1 | .854 |
| Persuasive 2 | .817 |

achievements as measured by high school grades and self-reports of writing ability obtained from the Student Descriptive Questionnaire (SDQ), or both. The SDQ item 50 is a self-rating of ability in creative writing; the SDQ item 60 is a self-rating of ability in written expression (see Appendix C).

Unfortunately, there appears to be more differentiation with respect to topic within mode than there is among modes. For example, there appears to be a stronger relationship between the multiple-choice test scores and the first topic in the narrative mode. This relationship, however, does not carry over to the second topic in the narrative mode. Almost all topics show proportionately greater association with test scores than they do with grades. On the whole there is little external evidence for the discriminant validity of the mode factors. Given the dominance of the standardized writing ability factor, it should come as no surprise that external variables show little in the way of systematic differential relationships.

## Conclusions from factor analyses

The results of this analytic factor study suggest the following:
- While there is one dominant writing ability factor that explains about 78 percent of the common variance, there are definable subfactors based on writing topics and, to a lesser extent, mode of expression. The presence of mode factors was

*Table 7.5. Higher-order factor solution with six topic factors and one general writing ability factor*

| Variables/readers | Factor 1 | Factor 2 | Factor 3 | Factor 4 | Factor 5 | Factor 6 |
|---|---|---|---|---|---|---|
| Narrative 1, R1 | .712 | — | — | — | — | — |
| Narrative 1, R2 | .793 | — | — | — | — | — |
| Narrative 1, R3 | .650 | — | — | — | — | — |
| Narrative 2, R1 | — | .741 | — | — | — | — |
| Narrative 2, R2 | — | .790 | — | — | — | — |
| Narrative 2, R3 | — | .635 | — | — | — | — |
| Expository 1, R1 | — | — | .795 | — | — | — |
| Expository 1, R2 | — | — | .748 | — | — | — |
| Expository 1, R3 | — | — | .820 | — | — | — |
| Expository 2, R1 | — | — | — | .789 | — | — |
| Expository 2, R2 | — | — | — | .737 | — | — |
| Expository 2, R3 | — | — | — | .792 | — | — |
| Persuasive 1, R1 | — | — | — | — | .785 | — |
| Persuasive 1, R2 | — | — | — | — | .872 | — |
| Persuasive 1, R3 | — | — | — | — | .770 | — |
| Persuasive 2, R1 | — | — | — | — | — | .826 |
| Persuasive 2, R2 | — | — | — | — | — | .817 |
| Persuasive 2, R3 | — | — | — | — | — | .683 |

*Factor intercorrelations*

| | | | | | | |
|---|---|---|---|---|---|---|
| Factor 1 | 1.0 | | | | | |
| Factor 2 | .689 | 1.0 | | | | |
| Factor 3 | .678 | .695 | 1.0 | | | |
| Factor 4 | .662 | .679 | .668 | 1.0 | | |
| Factor 5 | .591 | .605 | .596 | .581 | 1.0 | |
| Factor 6 | .579 | .593 | .584 | .570 | .509 | 1.0 |

*Loadings of first-order (topic) factor on second-order (general) factor*

| Topic factor | General factor |
|---|---|
| Narrative 1 | .820 |
| Narrative 2 | .840 |
| Expository 1 | .827 |
| Expository 2 | .807 |
| Persuasive 1 | .720 |
| Persuasive 2 | .706 |

*Note*: GFI = .898; RMSR = .061; $X^2$ = 271.67; *df* = 129.0; *p* = 0.0.

## Table 7.6. Factor structure extension

| Extension variables | Factor 1 | Factor 2 | Factor 3 | Factor 4 | Factor 5 | Factor 6 |
|---|---|---|---|---|---|---|
| SDQ 50[a] | .2029 | .2688 | .2021 | .2241 | .2202 | .2962 |
| SDQ 60[b] | .2407 | .2727 | .2481 | .2543 | .2040 | .2463 |
| English grade[c] | .2131 | .2983 | .2643 | .2993 | .3316 | .3217 |
| HSGPA[d] | .2108 | .2586 | .2402 | .3102 | .3954 | .2982 |
| SAT-V | .5843 | .4297 | .4870 | .4782 | .4432 | .3838 |
| SAT-M | .3798 | .2612 | .3242 | .3375 | .3941 | .2725 |
| TSWE | .6632 | .5212 | .5754 | .5384 | .5389 | .4370 |
| ECT | .6498 | .4730 | .4960 | .5121 | .5677 | .4474 |

a. Student self-report of creative writing ability.
b. Student self-report of written expression ability.
c. Student self-report of latest high school English grade.
d. Derived from student self-reports of latest high school grade in six course areas.

primarily due to differences between essays written in the persuasive mode and essays written in the narrative and expository modes. This mode difference is relatively small and may in part be an artifact of the difference in administration conditions between the persuasive mode and the other discourse modes.

▪ Factor models that took into consideration topic variance provided the best fit to the data. This is unfortunate in that a student could appear to be a good writer given one topic and a mediocre writer given an alternative topic within the same mode. Correlations between topic factors suggest that there was slightly less correlation between topic variance within the narrative mode compared with the expository mode.

▪ Factor extension results show that the first topic in the narrative mode ("Family Traditions") tended to have the higher correlations with multiple-choice measures of writing ability. This result suggests that a familiar topic, administered under controlled conditions, is most similar to standardized measures of writing ability.

# 8. Special analyses

Several special issues were of interest that either were not completely resolved in the analyses reported so far or required some special arrangement of data.

## *Multitrait-multimethod analysis*

These special multitrait-multimethod (MTMM) analyses were intended to explore even further than did the confirmatory factor analyses (see Chapter 7) questions concerning what the various writing assessments measure. We had available three different methods of measurement: non-essay (or multiple-choice) methods, essay methods, and instructors' ratings. Two traits (or skills) were of particular interest: general writing skills (GWS) and word and sentence skills (WSS). The non-essay measures—English Composition Test (ECT) and Test of Standard Written English (TSWE)—were hypothesized to measure word and sentence skills, as were the essay error counts and the instructors' ratings of mechanics skills (which emphasized word and sentence skills). The holistic scores and the instructors' ratings of discourse skills were hypothesized to measure more general writing skills. Under the multitrait-multimethod framework, validity is represented by agreement between two measures of the same trait (skill) obtained by different methods. Correlations between measures of the same trait (skill) conducted by different methods should be higher than correlations between different traits (skills) measured by different methods; they should also be higher than correlations between different traits measured by the same method.

Table 8.1 presents the results of the first MTMM analysis conducted. Figures in parentheses show how relationships have been adjusted for unreliability of measures. As noted in the table, the relationships shown are not representative of what would be obtained with the usual operational essay testing situation (that is, a single essay scored by two readers). Additionally, all relationships have been made positive even though error counts are negatively related to the other measures. Some of the relationships of Table 8.1 support the hypotheses, but others do not. For example, the instructors' ratings of students' word and sentence skills correlated better with ECT (.68) and TSWE (.63) scores than did their ratings of students' discourse skills (.42 and .39). This result supports the notion that non-essay measures such as the ECT and the TSWE assess primarily word and sentence skills, as logic would suggest, because both the ECT and the TSWE are limited to questions about such skills. Moreover, the instructors' ratings of discourse skills tend to correlate slightly better with holistic essay scores (.54) than they do with error counts (.50).

The second MTMM analysis (Table 8.2) rec-

*Table 8.1. First multitrait-multimethod analysis (using total essay scores)*

| Methods | Traits[a] (skills) | Non-essay WSS (ECT) | Non-essay WSS (TSWE) | Essay WSS (errors) | Essay GWS (holistic) | Ratings WSS | Ratings GWS |
|---|---|---|---|---|---|---|---|
| Non-essay (ECT) | WSS | 1.00 | | | | | |
| Non-essay (TSWE) | WSS | .87 (.96) | 1.00 | | | | |
| Essay (error counts)[b] | WSS | .63 (.68) | .69 (.76) | 1.00 | | | |
| Essay (holistic scores)[b] | GWS | .66 (.74) | .71 (.81) | .79 (.87) | 1.00 | | |
| Instructors' ratings | WSS | .55 (.68) | .50 (.63) | .48 (.59) | .58 (.73) | 1.00 | |
| | GWS | .34 (.42) | .31 (.39 | .40 (.50) | .43 (.54) | .49 (.69) | 1.00 |

*Note*: Based on Sample D. Figures in parentheses are corrected for unreliability of measures, using the following reliability estimates:

| Measure | Reliability |
|---|---|
| ECT | .92 |
| TSWE | .88 |
| Error counts | .93 |
| Holistic scores | .90 |
| Instructors' ratings | .70 |

a. WSS = word and sentence skills; GWS = general writing skills.
b. These essay measures are based on all six essays written for the project and all nine scorings of those essays. Accordingly, the relationships shown are not representative of operational situations where there is commonly only a single essay and two scorings of it. Operational essay scores would yield much lower correlations than those shown.

ognizes the three different essay modes as different methods. Results are similar to those of Table 8.1, but the across-mode comparisons allow for more precise analysis. Note that all figures are adjusted for the reliability of variables. Convergent validity of the narrative and the expository essay holistic scores is demonstrated by the high (.96) adjusted correlation between these two. But convergent validity is not clearly demonstrated for the persuasive essay holistic scores. The correlations between persuasive essay holistic scores and narrative or expository essay holistic scores are much less (.70 and .77) than the .96 correlation between narrative and expository essay holistic scores. And these correlations are not always higher than different skill/different method correlations. The best explanation for these results is that the persuasive essays measure skills dif-

ferent from those measured by narrative and expository essays. This was the same conclusion reached in the confirmatory factor analyses.

The most surprising result from both Tables 8.1 and 8.2 is in the correlations between the non-essay measures (TSWE and ECT) and the essay error counts. We had expected that the non-essay measures would correlate better with the error counts than with the holistic scores. But it turned out that the holistic scores correlated better with ECT and TSWE scores than did the error counts. In fact, for all essay types the holistic scores correlated better with ECT and TSWE scores than did the error counts. The holistic scores for narrative essays correlated much better with ECT and TSWE than with the error counts. The holistic scores for expository essays correlated slightly better with the ECT and TSWE scores

## Table 8.2. Second multitrait-multimethod analysis (using essay scores within mode)

| Method | Traits[a] (skills) | Non-essay ECT WSS | Non-essay TSWE WSS | Narrative essays Errors WSS | Narrative essays Holistic GWS | Expository essays Errors WSS | Expository essays Holistic GWS | Persuasive essays Errors WSS | Persuasive essays Holistic GWS | Instructors' ratings Mechanics WSS | Instructors' ratings Discourse GWS |
|---|---|---|---|---|---|---|---|---|---|---|---|
| Non-essay (ECT)[b] | WSS | 1.00 | | | | | | | | | |
| Non-essay (TSWE)[b] | WSS | .96 | 1.00 | | | | | | | | |
| Narrative essays (errors)[c] | WSS | .58[e] | .66[e] | 1.00 | | | | | | | |
| Narrative essays (holistic)[c] | GWS | .80[f] | .89[f] | .80[g] | 1.00 | | | | | | |
| Expository essays (errors)[c] | WSS | .64[e] | .70[e] | .64[e] | .78[f] | 1.00 | | | | | |
| Expository essays (holistic)[c] | GWS | .67[f] | .75[f] | .75[f] | .96[e] | .65[g] | 1.00 | | | | |
| Persuasive essays (errors)[c] | WSS | .51[e] | .52[e] | .52[e] | .67[f] | .53[e] | .71[f] | 1.00 | | | |
| Persuasive essays (holistic)[c] | GWS | .60[f] | .61[f] | .47[f] | .70[e] | .54[f] | .77[e] | .78[g] | 1.00 | | |
| Instructors' ratings (mechanics)[d] | WSS | .68[e] | .63[e] | .42[e] | .65[f] | .51[e] | .63[f] | .59[e] | .75[f] | 1.00 | |
| Instructors' ratings (discourse)[d] | GWS | .42[f] | .39[f] | .48[f] | .58[e] | .44[f] | .52[e] | .36[f] | .41[e] | .69[g] | 1.00 |

a. WSS = word and sentence skills; GWS = general writing skills.
b. Reliability of the ECT for this sample was estimated at .92 and that of the TSWE at .88.
c. Reliability of essay scores estimated as follows:

| Narrative essays | | Expository essays | | Persuasive essays | |
|---|---|---|---|---|---|
| Error count | .81 | Error count | .91 | Error count | .80 |
| Holistic score | .73 | Holistic score | .75 | Holistic score | .80 |

d. Reliability of instructors' ratings was assumed to be .70.
e. Correlation between measures of the same skills measured by different methods.
f. Correlation between measures of different skills measured by different methods.
g. Correlation between measures of different skills measured by the same method.

than did the error counts of these essays. The hypothesis that ECT and TSWE measure primarily word and sentence skills was not supported by these comparisons. These analyses suggest that tests that contain only sentence-level questions may measure more than their appearance would imply.

## Specific error counts as predictors

The unexpected observations in the MTMM analyses raised the question of how specific types of error counts may relate to holistic scores and non-essay assessments. Table 8.3 shows observed and corrected correlations between the six types of

## Table 8.3. Specific error counts as predictors of total holistic, ECT, and TSWE scores (Sample D)

| Specific error count | Observed correlation with | | | Corrected correlation with | | |
|---|---|---|---|---|---|---|
| | Holistic score | ECT | TSWE | Holistic score | ECT | TSWE |
| Grammar | .68 | .57 | .66 | .79 | .66 | .78 |
| Usage/diction | .72 | .58 | .60 | .83 | .66 | .70 |
| Sentence structure | .66 | .48 | .51 | .77 | .56 | .60 |
| GUSS errors | .79 | .63 | .69 | .87 | .68 | .76 |
| Punctuation | .45 | .35 | .28 | .54 | .42 | .34 |
| Spelling | .54 | .32 | .37 | .58 | .34 | .40 |
| Capitalization, etc. | .40 | .24 | .31 | .50 | .29 | .39 |
| PSC errors | .61 | .40 | .41 | .68 | .44 | .46 |
| Total errors | .79 | .57 | .61 | .86 | .61 | .67 |

*Note*: All correlations are negative.

error counts conducted and the essay and non-essay assessments. The total holistic score correlated best (.83) with the usage/diction error count and least (.50) with the capitalization, etc., count. This result would suggest that essay readers are most influenced by usage/diction errors, though the grammar and sentence structure relationships are not much lower (.79 and .77). Strong relationships with the last three error counts would not be expected, since the ECT and the TSWE do not test these skills and since holistic readers are not instructed to emphasize these factors when scoring.

## Analysis of ECT essays

In the 141 cases of Sample C, 42 cases had holistic essay scores based on the 20-minute essays included as a part of the December ETC administration. As another essay versus non-essay comparison, it was possible to compare these 20-minute essays with SAT-verbal, TSWE, and ECT scores as predictors of the writing performance,

course grade, and instructors' ratings outcomes (Table 8.4). Only one of the correlations with the ECT essay score was statistically significant—the correlation (.37) with the sum of the narrative and expository scores. Most of the other predictions in Table 8.4 were statistically significant, however. The TSWE achieved the most significant predictions. Only one outcome, the instructors' ratings of discourse skills, failed to yield a significant correlation with any predictor.

A particularly interesting observation from Table 8.4 is that the ECT score, which includes the 20-minute essay, predicted outcomes less well than did the TSWE. This result is most probably associated with the greater difficulty of the ECT, which tends to restrict its range in some samples and thus to attenuate correlations.

## Standardized predictor weights

Previous prediction analyses focused on multiple correlations and the incremental validity of predictor variables, but another issue is the weight

## Table 8.4. ECT 20-minute essay as predictor of college freshman writing performance in sample of 42 cases

| College freshman measure (outcome) | Correlation of outcome with ECT essay score | Correlation of outcome with | | |
|---|---|---|---|---|
| | | TSWE | ECT[a] | SAT-V |
| Total of six essay scores | .35 | .65* | .53* | .47* |
| Narrative + expository essay scores | .37* | .57* | .51* | .41* |
| Narrative + persuasive essay scores | .32 | .62* | .51* | .50* |
| Expository + persuasive essay scores | .32 | .66* | .51* | .44* |
| Freshman English course grade | .22 | .37* | .31 | .29 |
| Word and sentence skill rating | .14 | .40* | .35 | .26 |
| Discourse skill rating | .12 | .35 | .23 | .20 |
| Writing skill rating | .14 | .41* | .31 | .24 |

* $p < .01$.
a. Based on combined 40-minute multiple-choice test and 20-minute essay score.

## Table 8.5. Standardized weights for combinations of essay and non-essay tests as predictors of writing performance (Sample A)

| | Writing performance criteria[a] | | | | | | | | | | | |
|---|---|---|---|---|---|---|---|---|---|---|---|---|
| | WP1 | | WP2 | | WP3 | | WP4 | | WP5 | | WP6 | |
| Predictors | $R$ | beta | $R$ | beta | $R$ | beta | $R$ | beta | $R$ | beta | $R$ | beta |
| TSWE | .61 | .46 | .64 | .47 | .63 | .50 | .65 | .49 | .64 | .46 | .65 | .49 |
| SAT-V | | .20 | | .22 | | .19 | | .20 | | .22 | | .22 |
| TSWE | .64 | .46 | .64 | .47 | .63 | .48 | .65 | .50 | .64 | .47 | .65 | .50 |
| SAT-V | | .21 | | .22 | | .20 | | .21 | | .25 | | .23 |
| SAT-M | | −.03 | | .00 | | −.02 | | −.04 | | −.06 | | −.03 |
| TSWE | .69 | .29 | .75 | .30 | .74 | .31 | .77 | .36 | .74 | .30 | .75 | .36 |
| SAT-V | | .13 | | .14 | | .08 | | .12 | | .22 | | .17 |
| SAT-M | | −.03 | | .05 | | .02 | | −.05 | | −.09 | | −.02 |
| Essay[b] | | .39(N1) | | .44(N2) | | .46(E1) | | .47(E2) | | .43(P1) | | .40(P2) |

a. The criterion variable is the sum of five essays, excluding the essay used as a predictor.
b. The sum of three reader scores. The specific essay used is indicated in parentheses.

## Table 8.6. Standardized weights for combinations of essay and non-essay tests as predictors of course grade (Sample A)

| Predictors | R | beta | R | beta | R | beta | R | beta | R | beta | R | beta |
|---|---|---|---|---|---|---|---|---|---|---|---|---|
| | | | | | Multiple correlations and beta weights for prediction of course grade | | | | | | | |
| TSWE | .46 | .19 | .46 | .19 | .46 | .19 | .46 | .19 | .46 | .19 | .46 | .19 |
| SAT-V | | .31 | | .31 | | .31 | | .31 | | .31 | | .31 |
| TSWE | .47 | .20 | .47 | .20 | .47 | .20 | .47 | .20 | .47 | .20 | .47 | .20 |
| SAT-V | | .35 | | .35 | | .35 | | .35 | | .35 | | .35 |
| SAT-M | | −.09 | | .09 | | −.09 | | −.09 | | −.09 | | −.09 |
| TSWE | .52 | .08 | .53 | .09 | .49 | .13 | .53 | .12 | .59 | .04 | .58 | .08 |
| SAT-V | | .30 | | .30 | | .30 | | .29 | | .32 | | .30 |
| SAT-M | | −.08 | | −.05 | | −.07 | | −.09 | | −.12 | | −.08 |
| Essay[a] | | .27(N1) | | .29(N2) | | .18(E1) | | .28(E2) | | .41(P1) | | .38(P2) |

a. The sum of three reader scores. The specific essay used is indicated in parentheses.

## Table 8.7. Student self-reports as predictors of writing performance and English course outcomes

| | Correlations with college outcomes[a] | | |
|---|---|---|---|
| Predictors | Writing performance[b] | Freshman English grade | Writing skill—instructor |
| *Student self-reports* | | | |
| High school rank | .22 | .19 | .21 |
| High school GPA | .31 | .30 | .31 |
| High school English grade | .31 | .32 | .31 |
| Writing skill—student | .36 | .26 | .30 |
| *Test scores* | | | |
| SAT-V | .50 | .42 | .42 |
| TSWE | .61 | .40 | .48 |

*Note*: N = 200.
a. All correlations are significant at the .01 level.
b. Sum of six essay scores.

that variables receive in prediction. Table 8.5 shows the standardized weights (beta weights) obtained when three non-essay measures were combined with an essay to predict writing performance criteria. Also given are multiple correlations ($R$'s) for each predictor set. For all writing performance criteria, the essay received the greatest weight, though the TSWE and SAT-verbal scores also received substantial weight. As expected, the SAT-mathematical score did not figure importantly in predictions of writing performance.

Table 8.6 shows the same kind of analysis but with the course grade used as the criterion. Here it is seen that the SAT-verbal score receives the heaviest weight except when the persuasive essays are used in the prediction. The heavier weight for the persuasive essays may simply reflect the proximity in time between grade assignment and completion of the persuasive essays; on the other hand, it may suggest that the persuasive essays measure abilities that are closer to what instructors regard as most important.

## Self-reports as predictors

For a sample of 200 cases it was possible to examine information obtained from the Student Descriptive Questionnaire for predictive potential. The same three criteria were used as in previous

### Table 8.8. Marginal cost of alternative writing assessments

| Essay type | Topic | Number of readings | Reading time (minutes)[a] | Reading cost[b] | Validity[c] ECT | ECT + essay | Marginal cost[d] |
|---|---|---|---|---|---|---|---|
| Narrative | "Family Traditions" | 1 | 1.82 | $ .76 | .62 | .68 | $ .13 |
| | | 2 | 3.64 | 1.52 | | .71 | .25 |
| | | 3 | 5.46 | 2.28 | | .72 | .76 |
| | "Significant Event" | 1 | 1.82 | .76 | .66 | .72 | .13 |
| | | 2 | 3.64 | 1.52 | | .74 | .38 |
| | | 3 | 5.46 | 2.28 | | .75 | .76 |
| Expository | "Status Symbols" | 1 | 1.30 | .54 | .67 | .78 | .05 |
| | | 2 | 2.61 | 1.08 | | .81 | .18 |
| | | 3 | 7.83 | 1.62 | | .82 | .54 |
| | "Cornerstone" | 1 | 1.30 | .54 | .66 | .74 | .07 |
| | | 2 | 2.61 | 1.08 | | .77 | .18 |
| | | 3 | 3.91 | 1.62 | | .79 | .27 |
| Persuasive | "Drinking and Driving" | 1 | 3.53 | 1.47 | .66 | .74 | .18 |
| | | 2 | 7.06 | 2.94 | | .76 | 1.47 |
| | | 3 | 10.59 | 4.41 | | .76 | — |
| | "Book Censorship" | 1 | 3.53 | 1.47 | .66 | .72 | .24 |
| | | 2 | 7.06 | 2.94 | | .75 | .49 |
| | | 3 | 10.59 | 4.41 | | .76 | 1.47 |

a. Per examinee based on reading rates of 46 per hour for expository essays, 33 for narrative, and 17 for persuasive.
b. Per examinee based on reader cost rate of $25/hour, including transportation, meals, and support services.
c. Based on Sample D.
d. Of each added unit of validity.

analyses: writing performance, freshman English course grade, and instructors' ratings of writing skill. Table 8.7 presents the results of this analysis. Predictive correlations for SAT-verbal and TSWE scores in the same sample are included for comparison. The self-reports would suggest that students' perceptions of their own writing skills provide a moderate prediction of later writing performance but that the self-reported high school English grade is a better predictor of college English grades. For all three criteria, test scores provided better predictions than did student self-reports.

## Marginal cost of essay assessment

Table 8.8 gives the results of an analysis of incremental validity and marginal costs for the essay assessments used in this investigation. The marginal cost indicated in the last column represents, under certain assumptions, the cost of each additional unit of validity. To take an example from Table 8.8, the validity of the ECT for predicting the first writing performance criterion (excluding the first narrative essay) is .62. When the first narrative essay was used as an additional predictor, the multiple correlation increased to .68. There was an increase of 6 units of validity, and this additional (marginal) validity is estimated to cost 76 cents per examinee, ignoring costs for development and administration of the essay. Thus, the marginal cost for each of these additional units of validity was 13 cents per examinee. When two readings were used, the multiple correlation increased to 71 cents, an increment of 3 units of validity, but the second reading cost an additional 76 cents per examinee. So the marginal cost of the second reading was 25 cents per examinee. The third reading yielded only a single additional unit of validity, and as a result, the marginal cost was high (76 cents per examinee).

The lowest marginal cost figure occurred when the first expository essay ("Status Symbols") was used with one reading. Moreover, the multiple correlation attained using this essay (.78) was higher than that for any other essay with either one or two readings. Only the second expository essay ("Cornerstone") yielded a higher multiple correlation (.79), and that occurred for three readings. Since readers were nested within essay type, these differences across essay types could be due to reader differences.

## 9. Summary and conclusions

Using as a model a previous study of writing ability (Godshalk et al. 1966), we conducted a similar investigation in collaboration with six postsecondary institutions. Though the earlier study used secondary schools as collaborators, it was reasoned that postsecondary institutions would produce a better base of data—especially if these institutions participated in the College Board Admissions Testing Program (ATP). Through contacts with English departments in a wide range of institutions, a number were identified who were interested in a collaborative investigation. From these we selected six institutions based on their degree of participation in the ATP, their geographic location, and their selectivity. Because a high degree of selectivity in admissions would restrict the range of data obtained, not more than one highly selective institution was wanted. These institutions were selected: Brandeis University, Rutgers University at Camden, Spelman College, Texas A&M University, the University of California at Los Angeles, and the University of Vermont.

Representatives of the English departments in the selected institutions were invited to a planning conference held in August 1984, at which the following arrangements for the study were made. Approximately 50 students in each insti-

tution would write six essays as a part of the regular freshman English course instruction. The six essays would be of three types—narrative, expository, and persuasive—with two essays of each type. It was agreed that the narrative and expository essays would be written in class (in about 45 minutes for each) but that a sequential procedure would be used for the persuasive essays. For these the students would first prepare drafts, then discuss them with their teacher or peers, and complete them outside of class. These essays would be scored centrally by English teachers from other institutions. Instructors participating in the study would provide course grades and ratings of the writing ability of the students who wrote essays. It was agreed that even though instructors would be identified with data collected from their classes, no analyses within class or within institution would be conducted.

The collected data exceeded expectations, with approximately 350 students participating. To be included in the analyses, however, a student was required to write all six essays. After students were excluded who had not written all six essays or who could not be matched with College Board data, a total of 270 complete cases were available for analysis. Of these, 267 cases had data on all variables of interest; this group was labeled Sample A. For special analyses, three subsets of data were identified: Sample B was made up of 210 students who had English Composition Test (ECT) scores. Some of the Sample B ECT scores were approximate because they were based on old test forms administered expecially for the study (new forms could not be used for test security reasons) or because statistical procedures were used to remove essay components from the scores. Sample C comprised 141 cases, all with ECT scores from regular administrations; some of these scores included essay components. Sample D (94 cases) had only ECT scores from regular administrations based entirely on multiple-choice tests.

## Study objectives and outcomes

The first objective of this research investigation was to provide a better understanding of how essay assessments of writing skills differ from non-essay assessments of writing skills. We found that they differ in several ways. Essay assessments tend to be less reliable than multiple-choice measures, as has long been known, and these problems in reliability can be alleviated only through multiple essays or through the combination of essay and non-essay measures. Essay assessments are more costly than multiple-choice assessments, even when they are limited to single essays, but this is not a new discovery, either. Other differences between these two kinds of assessment were observed in our analyses of predictive and construct validity.

Because of the importance of reliability to validity outcomes, reliability should be considered first. We estimated the reliabilities of single essays read once to be in the range .36–.46; read twice, in the range .47–.57; and read thrice, in the range .53–.62 with small variations for specific types of essays. Less variable reliabilities, in the range .51–.53, were obtained for two essays each read only once. Using six essays, each read three times, it was possible to achieve reliabilities similar to those common for multiple-choice tests like the TSWE and the ECT (.84–.88 for TSWE and .88–.92 for ECT in national samples). The

predictive validity analyses showed essay assessments to be reasonably valid despite their low reliability.

Table 9.1 shows comparisons of average validities for essay and non-essay assessments. The criterion used for these validity comparisons was the sum of scores on five essays, each read by three independent readers, or the sum of 15 ratings of a student's writing performance. Where an essay was used as a predictor, that essay was always removed from the criterion to avoid an artificial inflation of validity. Since six different criteria were used (because six different essays were removed from each criterion), the figures shown in Table 9.1 are averages across these six criteria. The same six criteria were used for both the essay and the non-essay validities; thus, the comparison is not biased in any way by the criteria. The only bias involved in the comparison is that the non-essay measures (TSWE and ECT) were administered some time before the criterion data were collected (about one year for most students), while the essay assessment data were collected during the same semester (or quarter). These differences in proximity of time would attenuate the correlations for TSWE and ECT and maximize the correlations for essay tests because the essays being examined were written at about the same time as the criterion essays. Assuming that these differences in time proximity are relatively unimportant, Table 9.1 would suggest that multiple-choice tests of writing skill are roughly equivalent to single-essay tests as predictors— provided that the essays are read two or, preferable, three times.

An interesting result shown in Table 9.1 is that a 30-minute test, the TSWE, consistently outperformed a 1-hour test, the ECT, in the validity analyses. The ECT, however, includes a 20-minute essay in some administrations. Therefore, it is surprising to observe higher correlations for the TSWE. The reason for this anomaly is that the ECT is a relatively difficult test, most often re-

## Table 9.1. Comparison of essay and multiple-choice assessments of writing skill as predictors of writing performance criteria

| Sample | Average correlations with five-essay criteria | | | | |
| | Essay (1 reading) | Essay (2 readings) | Essay (3 readings) | TSWE | ECT |
|---|---|---|---|---|---|
| A | .54 | .61 | .64 | .62 | — |
| B | .55 | .62 | .64 | .62 | .60 |
| C | .56 | .63 | .66 | .68 | .62 |
| D | .57 | .64 | .68 | .70 | .66 |
| Average | .56 | .62 | .66 | .66 | .63 |

*Note:* Samples were developed as follows:

A. 267 cases having complete data on six essays and all other data except ECT scores.

B. 210 cases having complete data, but some ECT scores are approximate. No essay component is present in any ECT scores.

C. 141 cases based on regular administrations; some ECT scores contain essay components.

D. 94 cases based on regular all-multiple-choice ECT administrations; no essays are represented in any ECT scores.

quired by very selective institutions. Since the samples of students engaged for this study were purposely chosen so as to obtain a wide range of abilities, they represent a less able group than do those students who typically take the ECT. The lower ability of the sample tends to attenuate relationships for the more difficult ECT.

Further evidence of the differences and similarities of essay and non-essay assessments was obtained from construct validity analyses. Confirmatory factor analyses suggested that the specific essay topic used may define to some degree the construct measured. The best-fitting factor model was obtained when the six topics were posited to represent different factors. This finding is similar to that of Quellmalz et al. (1982), who concluded that "writing for different aims draws on different skill constructs"; but it is different in that in our data, specific topics (within different writing purposes) tended to relate to different factors. Additional construct validity analyses were conducted by means of multitrait-multimethod (MTMM) comparisons. For these analyses it was hypothesized that the more general writing skills

are those assessed through holistic scoring of essays and that word and sentence skills are those assessed through non-essay assessments or through error counts of essays. The word and sentence skills examined encompassed grammar, usage, and sentence structure but ignored punctuation, spelling, capitalization, and so forth. Three methods (non-essay, essay, and instructors' ratings) were used to assess the two skill constructs. The results of these MTMM analyses were contrary to expectation. Holistic scores correlated better with ECT and TSWE scores than did error counts, an outcome that failed to support the hypothesis that ECT and TSWE measure primarily word and sentence skills. The differences observed were not merely artifacts of reliability differences because those artifacts were controlled in the MTMM analyses.

To determine how the essay and the non-essay assessments might complement one another, which was the second objective of the project, validity analyses were also conducted for combinations of the two kinds of assessment. Table 9.2 summarizes these analyses, which were limited to Samples B and D because ECT scores were not available for Sample A and because some of the ECT scores of Sample C were already based on combinations of essay and non-essay scores. Table 9.2 indicated that very good predictions of writing ability may be made through combinations of essay and non-essay assessments. The average correlations for these combinations are somewhat higher than those possible using either essay or non-essay assessments in isolation. For example, a one-reading essay assessment used alone correlated only about .56 (average of Samples B and D in Table 9.1) with the writing performance criteria, while the combination of a one-reading essay assessment with the ECT yielded a multiple correlation of about .71 (average of Samples B and D in Table 9.2). This represents an incremental validity for the ECT of .15. The comparative utility of the non-essay assessment decreased, of course, as more readings of the

essay were made. With two readings the ECT increment was reduced to .11, and with three readings, to .09. Similar increments were observed for the TSWE. When both the TSWE and the ECT were used in combination with an essay assessment, little increase in the multiple correlation occurred. Thus, neither the TSWE nor the ECT made substantial contributions to the prediction independent of each other. (See Appendix E, note 8.)

The third project objective, to explore ways to reduce the cost and enhance the effectiveness of essay assessments, was realized through an analysis of validity and marginal cost. That is, we sought to determine the cost as well as the benefit of essay assessments as adjuncts to non-essay assessments. To determine what precise combinations of essay and non-essay assessments are optimal, the concept of marginal cost was used.

The analysis of marginal costs supported the use of expository essays of the type used in this investigation, and it suggested that additional readings of essays contribute relatively little to validity when essays are used in consort with a multiple-choice assessment like the ECT. Although small increments in validity are possible with additional readings, the marginal cost of these additional readings is relatively high. Consequently, one way to reduce the cost of essay assessments is to combine them with a multiple-choice assessment and to limit the number of readings as much as is acceptable. Braun (1986) has recently shown that essay scores that have been calibrated, or statistically adjusted, for reader idiosyncrasies are more reliable. This calibration of scores represents another approach to enhancing the effectiveness without increasing the costs of essay assessments.

The final objective of the project, to explore ways to strengthen the relationship between the assessment process and the instructional process, was realized implicitly. The project demonstrated that it is possible for the assessment to

## Table 9.2. Essay and non-essay assessment combinations as predictors of writing performance criteria

| | Average multiple correlations with writing performance criteria[a] | | |
|---|---|---|---|
| Sample | Essay + ECT | Essay + TSWE | Essay + ECT + TSWE |
| *Essay with 1 reading* | | | |
| B | .69 | .70 | .72 |
| D | .73 | .76 | .76 |
| *Essay with 2 readings* | | | |
| B | .72 | .73 | .74 |
| D | .76 | .77 | .78 |
| *Essay with 3 readings* | | | |
| B | .73 | .74 | .75 |
| D | .77 | .78 | .79 |

a. Essay used for these analyses was 45 minutes in length; ECT is a 60-minute test, and TSWE is a 30-minute test.

incorporate aspects of writing currently emphasized in writing pedagogy: writing for a variety of purposes and audiences and writing based on reflection and revision. The complications involved in including multiple samples of writing developed over time may be difficult to manage in large-scale assessment. If an assessment, however, can be designed to draw its samples from work completed as part of a writing course, as was true in this project, the complications of large-scale assessments are avoided. The project thus demonstrated some ways in which assessment and instruction can be integrated.

## Comparisons with previous research

The results obtained in this investigation compare reasonably well with those obtained by Godshalk et al. over 20 years ago. Their five-essay criterion was estimated to have a reliability of .84; our six-essay criterion was estimated to have a reliability of .88. Some larger differences in reliability estimates did occur for fewer numbers of essays. For example, Coffman (1966) reported a reliability of .26 for a single essay read by one reader. Our estimate for that situation was .42. For a single essay read twice—the most common situation—Coffman (1966) reported an estimate of .38, whereas we estimated a reliability of .53 for that situation. These differences in reliability estimates may be attributable to the use of a 3-point score scale in the Coffman study in contrast to the 6-point scale that we used. Differences in reliabilities could also have resulted from the different essay types used and the differences in the time allowed. The Coffman study used two 40-minute and three 20-minute essays. Our essays were longer: 45 minutes for the timed essays and unlimited time for the persuasive essays.

The relationships between essay and multiple-choice measures of writing skill obtained in the Godshalk et al. study and our study are similar.

In three samples Godshalk et al. observed correlations from .64 to .71 between usage and sentence correction tests (multiple-choice) and their five-essay criterion. In four samples our observed correlations between a similar usage and sentence correction test (TSWE) and our six-essay criterion ranged from .63 to .72. Thus, while the emphases in writing instruction have changed over the past 20 years, the relation between essay performance and the knowledge tested by usage and sentence correction items appears not to have changed very much.

In a more recent study Breland and Gaynor (1979) obtained a correlation of .76 between the sum of scores for three essays and the sum of three TSWE scores. One explanation for this difference in results may be the kinds of essays used. In the Breland and Gaynor study all three essays were expository, and thus scores on them would tend to be more additive than would scores on widely different types of essays like those used in our study.

Other writers have also reported the use of error counts. Hull (1984) emphasized the difficulty in obtaining accurate error counts, even though it is commonly assumed that the counting of errors is a simple task. Our experiences buttress Hull's observation because we found that about 16 percent of our error count scores had to be adjudicated by a third reading in order to attain respectable reliabilities. Moss et al. (1982) correlated error counts with holistic scores of the same essays in a sample of tenth-grade students and obtained an observed correlation of .42 (corrected to .72 when reliability was considered). This correlation is much less than the correlation of .79 (corrected to .87) obtained in our study. A careful examination of the Moss et al. procedures shows that their error counts were primarily of spelling, capitalization, and punctuation—not grammar, usage, and sentence structure, which were used here. An examination of our correlations between holistic scores and error counts similar to those used in the Moss et al. study shows correlations similar to those obtained by them. Punctuation errors correlated $-.45$ with holistic scores, spelling errors $-.54$, and capitalization, and so forth, $-.40$.

We also agree with Moss et al. in a general observation. As did the results of their study, the results of this one "illustrate again the complexity of measuring different aspects of writing skill." But while Moss et al.—as well as Quellmalz et al.—emphasized the differences between different *types* of writing, we would like to extend that complexity even further by suggesting that not only are different types of writing important, but the specific topics assigned may elicit different skills or knowledge even within the same type of writing.

Despite these complexities, the results of this study—as well as those obtained by Godshalk et al.—show that the best estimates of students' writing abilities are obtained through tests that combine essay assessments and multiple-choice assessments. The optimum amounts of testing time to allocate to each type of assessment have not been established, but an allocation of 45 minutes to the essay and 30 minutes to the multiple-choice test worked well in this investigation. Statistical comparisons do not show a clear advantage to the longer essay, but most teachers of English composition prefer it.

Beyond these predictive advantages of combined assessments, there is also a practical advantage. The multiple-choice component provides a means through which different forms of tests can be equated, so that examinees taking different forms of a test can be assigned equivalent scores. No comparable technique is possible when only essay assessments are used.

## Appendix A: The writing tasks

Narrative 1

Please PRINT the following information:

Name:_____/_____/_____
　　　　　　　　　(last)　　　　　　　　(first)　　　　(middle initial)

Birthdate:_____/_____/_____
　　　　　　　(month)　　　　　　　　(day)　　　　　　　(year)

### WRITING ASSIGNMENT
(Suggested time:　45 minutes)

　　　In the class time allowed, you are to
plan and write a paper on the topic presented
on the reverse side of this page.　To be sure
you have enough space in the booklet for your
paper, you should avoid skipping lines,
writing in excessively large letters, or
leaving wide margins.　You may use the extra
space below the topic to make notes for
yourself before you write or while you are
writing.　You are to write for an audience
that includes your classmates and instructor.

## TOPIC

Think of a tradition you have lived with for several years. Consider, for example, particular ways of celebrating birthdays or spending summer vacations, longstanding customs you share with old friends, family traditions surrounding ethnic and religious holidays. Select one of these customs or traditions and describe it in detail, showing what it means to you.

## NOTES

Please <u>PRINT</u> the following information:

Name:_____/_____/_____
(last)                (first)         (middle initial)

Birthdate:_____/_____/_____
(month)         (day)         (year)

<u>WRITING ASSIGNMENT</u>
(Suggested time:  45 minutes)

In the class time allowed, you are to plan and write a paper on the topic presented on the reverse side of this page.  To be sure you have enough space in the booklet for your paper, you should avoid skipping lines, writing in excessively large letters, or leaving wide margins.  You may use the extra space below the topic to make notes for yourself before you write or while you are writing.  You are to write for an audience that includes your classmates and instructor.

## TOPIC

Some events in our lives are significant because they change us in an important way. Think of an event in your life that changed you. You might want to consider, for example, an event such as the first time you accomplished something that was important to you, the first time you realized you had a skill or an ambition that made you distinct from other people, or the first time you became aware of a prejudice or a misconception or discovered that someone you admired was imperfect. Write about one such event in your life, recalling it in such a way that your reader can understand why it was significant and how it changed you.

## NOTES

Please <u>PRINT</u> the following information:

Name:_____/_____/_____
                    (last)                    (first)              (middle initial)

Birthdate:_____/_____/_____
                    (month)                    (day)                    (year)

<u>WRITING ASSIGNMENT</u>
(Suggested time:  45 minutes)

    In the class time allowed, you are to plan and write a paper on the topic presented on the reverse side of this page.  To be sure you have enough space in the booklet for your paper, you should avoid skipping lines, writing in excessively large letters, or leaving wide margins.  You may use the extra space below the topic to make notes for yourself before you write or while you are writing.  You are to write for an audience that includes your classmates and instructor.

# TOPIC

Although fashions come and go, there is always a fashion, a status symbol, an object or a thing that people desire and want to have. For example, some people carry around large silver stereo radios or listen to cassette players through earphones. Some people must have a particular brand of sport shoe or jeans, and some must have a certain breed of dog or a particular kind of car.

Choose one object or thing that seems to lend prestige or importance to its owners. Then write a well-organized essay that describes the particular status that the object confers and explain why people seem to need and want such objects.

## NOTES

Please PRINT the following information:

Name:_____ / _____ / _____
             (last)                (first)      (middle initial)

Birthdate:_____ / _____ / _____
             (month)          (day)        (year)

## WRITING ASSIGNMENT
### (Suggested time:  45 minutes)

In the class time allowed, you are to plan and write a paper on the topic presented on the reverse side of this page.  To be sure you have enough space in the booklet for your paper, you should avoid skipping lines, writing in excessively large letters, or leaving wide margins.  You may use the extra space below the topic to make notes for yourself before you write or while you are writing.  You are to write for an audience that includes your classmates and instructor.

## TOPIC

The tradition of placing small articles in the cornerstone of a new building is an ancient one.  It is expected that when uncovered by some future generation, these articles will convey significant characteristics of the time and culture they represent.

Think of articles representative of our time—anything from commonplace objects to components of sophisticated inventions—that might be placed in the cornerstone of an important new building in your town or city. Choose one or more such articles and write a well-organized essay explaining what they signify about our time and culture.

## NOTES

## Reading and Writing Assignment

SOMETHING TO THINK ABOUT

Across the United States, automobile accidents are the major cause of death among 15- to 24-year-olds. Many of these accidents involve young drivers who have been drinking. In an attempt to deal with the problem, Congress has passed a law intended to establish 21 as the minimum drinking age across the country. Others have argued that the minimum driving age should be raised instead. Highway safety organizations, state police, and groups of private citizens have made various attempts to solve the problem. These have ranged from urging citizens to report drunk drivers on the highway to educating high school students about the role of alcohol in automobile accidents.

As a young person in the age group most affected by the problem discussed above and its proposed solutions, you probably have a great many ideas about the subject and about what would be most helpful in solving the problem.

As you work through the steps of this assignment, think carefully about proposed solutions to the problem, trying to discover the solution that you believe is most likely to work. You will be asked later in this assignment to write a paper in which you propose the solution you think is best. The process of writing this paper will help you and your instructor and classmates to clarify your thinking about the problem; further, the end result will be a written statement of your views, a statement that you can send, if you wish, to various groups and officials concerned about solving the problem. The views you express in your paper may thus contribute to an effective solution to this national problem.

WHAT YOU WILL BE ASKED TO DO

The assignment has several steps

o   Reading an article that will acquaint you with the problem and some solutions that have already been proposed.

o   Writing a first draft of a statement in which you argue for the best possible solution as you see it.

o   Discussing your first draft with your classmates and/or your instructor.

o   Rewriting your paper to improve it, incorporating what you have learned from discussions and from your own continued thinking about the problem.

You will be given detailed instructions for each step as you reach it.

Step 1:   Reading and thinking

As the first step toward developing the ideas for your statement, you are to read a newspaper article by Neal Peirce.  It was written shortly after Congress passed a law that threatens states with loss of highway funds if they fail to raise the minimum drinking age to 21.

Despite the article's slightly humorous tone, the issues it raises are serious ones.  Read it carefully, using your own experience and judgment to determine the value of Peirce's ideas.  When you have finished reading the article, think about

- o    The solution it proposes for the problem of drinking and driving among young people.
- o    The solution that Congress has tried to effect by passing the new law.
- o    Other attempts you know of to deal with the problem.
- o    The needs, attributes, and behavior of young people as they are related to the problem.

Then, decide what you think would be the best solution to the problem.  You will be asked to present this solution in the first draft of your paper.

Please PRINT the following information:

Name:_____/_____/_____
             (last)             (first)       (middle initial)

Birthdate:_____/_____/_____
           (month)        (day)        (year)

## Step 2: Writing the first draft
### (Suggested time: 45 minutes)

You have already read the Neil Peirce editorial "Let's Raise the Driving Age, Instead" and thought about the problem of drinking and driving among young adults. In the class time available today, you are to plan and to write the first draft of your statement on solving the problem.

At the end of the class, you will be asked to give this booklet to your instructor. The booklet will be returned to you within a few days. At that time your instructor or your classmates will respond to your writing, giving you suggestions to help improve your paper. You will also be given instructions on format and a date on which to turn in the finished version of your written statement. This finished version is the one that will be evaluated.

Read carefully the topic presented on the reverse side of this page. If you wish, use the extra space below the topic to plan your draft. Since you are writing a draft, you may want to leave extra-wide margins so that you will have room for notes to yourself later on about ideas that you want to add or present differently. You are not expected to write on all of the pages of this booklet, but you may use as much space as you need. You should work toward 2 to 4 typed pages as the length of the final version of your paper.

## TOPIC

You have read and thought about various ways of reducing the number of alcohol-related highway fatalities among young people. Drawing on your own experience and observation as well as what you have read, and expressing your ideas in a clear and organized manner, write a paper in which you show how the number of alcohol-related automobile accidents among young adults can best be reduced. Be sure to demonstrate why what you propose is likely to be effective.

Think of this paper as the first version of a statement you can eventually send to people who are in a position to do something to solve the problem. Although your paper will be read by your instructor and perhaps by your classsmates, you should address those individuals and groups that help make public policy. Remember that such people do not know you or your friends or your particular community.

You may cite Peirce's article or other
materials if you think doing so will
contribute to the force of your argument, but
you should not assume that your readers have
already read what you have.  If you decide to
cite other writers, or if you use statistical
information, you will need to provide
references in your final version so that your
readers can consult your sources if they wish
to do so.  In general, you should rely more on
careful reasoning, thoughtful suggestions, and
the testimony of your own experience and
observation than on evidence drawn from
outside sources.

Begin planning and writing your draft as soon
as you are ready.

<u>NOTES</u>

## Reading and Writing Assignment

SOMETHING TO THINK ABOUT

The right of school authorities to censor books used in the schools is an issue being debated in the courts now. At odds are two fundamental concepts:

o   The constitutional right of the citizen to express ideas without suppression by authorities

o   The traditional and legally upheld right of parents and those standing in place of parents (school boards, for example) to raise their child according to their religious and moral values

The basic and important nature of these concepts makes the controversy surrounding censorship highly emotional. Whether people defend censorship or oppose it, they fervently believe that their attitude is the right one.

You are one of the young people whose education has been affected by censorhsip, whether or not your local school board has actually banned books. You are also in a position to know what the demands of a high school education are and perhaps also what they should be. As you read the information provided to you on the censorship of textbooks and books available in school libraries, decide what your own attitude toward the problem is. You may be for the censorship of books used in the schools or against it, or you may see merit on both sides of the issue.

You will be asked later to offer constructive suggestions to the parents, teachers, school boards, and others who are trying to find a workable solution to the problem. Most of these people believe that establishing guidelines for the selection and use of books in the schools will go a long way tword solving the problem. But determining what those guidelines should be is a difficult task when the issues are so complex and so basic.

Before you write the final version of your paper, you will complete various assignments that are meant to help you think about the censorship of school books and clarify your own ideas about it. The final version of your paper is intended to be a statement that you can send, if you wish to do so, to local or state school officials or to the various organizations taking an active part in the efforts to resolve the controversy over censorship. Your ideas on the issue and on the ways to solve the problem will then be among those they consider as they weigh various proposals to resolve this local, state, and national dilemma reasonably and effectively.

WHAT YOU WILL BE ASKED TO DO

The assignment has several steps:

- o    Reading an article and excerpts from articles to acquaint you with the problem.
- o    Writing a first draft of a statement in which you present your ideas on the censorship of school books and offer your suggestions for solving the problem.
- o    Discussing your first draft with your classmates and/or your instructor.
- o    Rewriting your paper to improve it, incorporating what you have learned from discussions and from your own continued thinking about the issue.

You will be given detailed instructions for each step as you reach it.

Step 1:   Reading and thinking

The purpose of the collection of printed statements that you are to read for this assignment is to provide you with some background information about censorship of school books and some idea of the different opinions held.

1.   Read these statements carefully; as you read, note especially:

    o    The opinions people express and the reasons they give for holding those opinions
    o    Any suggestions offered in the articles to help solve the problem

2.   Then, evaluate what you have read:

    o    Are the reasons given appropriate in the light of your own experience and your ideas about education?
    o    What is your opinion of the relative value of each of the reasons given?

3.   Next, think about your own attitudes, your reasons for holding them, and the constructive suggestions you might make to those working on the problem of censorship.  You will later be asked to present these ideas in the first draft of your paper.

As you think about what you will write in your paper, consider the following questions:

o     What is your own attitude toward the issue?

o     What are the basic areas of conflict between those who wish to censor the books chosen for schools and those who do not?

o     What merits can you see in the arguments presented on each side?

o     What do you believe to be the most important issues to be resolved?

o     What compromise, if any, do you think people on each side should make to help solve the problem?

o     What suggestions can you offer that will ensure that the materials chosen will best serve the community, the schools, and the students?

Please <u>PRINT</u> the following information:

Name: _____ / _____ / _____
            (last)           (first)        (middle initial)

Birthdate: _____ / _____ / _____
          (month)        (day)        (year)

### Step 2:  Writing the first draft
### (Suggested time:  45 minutes)

You have already read a collection of statements on censorship of school books and considered your own and others' ideas about censorship and the various ways of dealing with the problems it presents.  In the class time available today, you are to plan and to write the first draft of your statement on the issue.

At the end of the class, you will be asked to give this booklet to your instructor.  The booklet will be returned to you within a few days.  At that time your instructor or your classmates will respond to your writing, giving you suggestions to help improve your paper.  You will also be given instructions on format and a date on which to turn in the finished version of your written statement.  This finished version is the one that will be evaluated.

Read carefully the topic presented on the reverse side of this page.  If you wish, use the extra space below the topic to plan your draft.  Since you are writing a draft, you may want to leave extra-wide margins so that you will have room for notes to yourself later on about ideas that you want to add or to present differently.  You are not expected to write on all of the pages of this booklet, but you may use as much space as you need.  You should work toward 2 to 4 typed pages as the length of the final version of your paper.

## TOPIC

Write a paper in which you offer constructive suggestions to those working to establish guidelines for choosing school books. Be sure to indicate why what you propose is likely to be effective and why you have proposed it. Remember that the people reading your paper may have had different experiences and hold different opinions. You will want to persuade them of the value of your ideas and the worth of your suggestions.

In presenting your ideas, draw upon:

- o     Your experience as a student and as a reader.
- o     Your knowledge of other students, their experiences and their attitudes.
- o     The information and insights gained from discussions, from the readings assigned, and from other sources.
- o     Your observations of the world around you.

Think of this paper as the first version of a statement you can eventually send to people who are involved in the controversy and are in a position to do something to solve the problem. Although your paper will be read by your instructor and perhaps by your classmates, you should address your ideas to those individuals and groups that are developing the guidelines. Remember that such people do not know you or your friends or even your particular school system or community.

You may cite the statements in the collection provided earlier if you think doing so will contribute to the force of your argument; the sources of the excerpts are listed on a separate page that your instructor will distribute to your class. However, you should not assume that your readers have already read what you have. If you decide to cite other writers, or if you use statistical information, you will need to provide references in your final version so that your readers can consult your sources if they wish to do so. In general, you should rely more on careful reasoning, thoughtful suggestions, and your own experiences as a student and a reader as well as your observation of the world around you than on evidence drawn from outside sources.

Begin planning and writing your draft as soon as you are ready.

NOTES

## Appendix B: Error count form and instructions

Essay #_____

Reader #_____

## *Error counts**

|  |  |  |  | Total |
|---|---|---|---|---|
| Grammar | _____ 5 | _____ 10 | _____ 15 | _____ |
| Usage/Diction | _____ 5 | _____ 10 | _____ 15 | _____ |
| Sentence Structure | _____ 5 | _____ 10 | _____ 15 | _____ |
| Punctuation | _____ 5 | _____ 10 | _____ 15 | _____ |
| Spelling | _____ 5 | _____ 10 | _____ 15 | _____ |
| Capitalization, Titles, Contractions, etc. | _____ 5 | _____ 10 | _____ 15 | _____ |

_____

* Place one tally mark (/) in the spaces indicated for each error of each type encountered. Record the total at the right.

# Grammar, diction, structure, and usage errors

The following list of errors and the accompanying sentences that illustrate them are not exhaustive; students make other errors that are sometimes too difficult to classify. Or, such errors may be a combination of two or more errors on this list. In doing the error count, you need merely record a tally mark in the appropriate space on the scoring sheet for each error you see. Do not place any marks on the actual essay.

## Being consistent

| | |
|---|---|
| Sequence of tenses | After he broke his arm, he is home for two weeks. |
| Shift of pronoun | If one is tense, they should try to relax. |
| Parallelism | She skis, plays tennis, and flying hang gliders. |
| Nonagreement | Ann and Sarah want to be a pilot. |
| Pronoun reference | Several people wanted the job, and he or she filled out the required application. |
| Subject-verb agreement | There is eight people on the shore. |

## Expressing ideas logically

| | |
|---|---|
| Coordination and subordination | Nancy has a rash, and she is probably allergic to something. |
| Logical comparison | Harry grew more vegetables than his neighbor's garden. |
| Modification and word order | Barking loudly, the tree had the dog's leash wrapped around it. |

## Being clear and precise

| | |
|---|---|
| Ambiguous and vague pronouns | In the newspaper they say that few people voted. |
| Diction | He circumvented the globe on his trip. |
| Wordiness | There are many problems in the contemporary world in which we live. |
| Unclear modification | If your car is parked here while not eating in the restaurant, it will be towed away. |

## Following conventions

| | |
|---|---|
| Pronoun case | He sat between you and I at the stadium. |
| Verb form | She had brung her lunch yesterday. |
| Idiom | Manuel had a different opinion towards her. |
| Comparison of modifiers | Of the sixteen executives, Meg makes more money. |
| Sentence fragment | Jane having to go home early. |
| Double negative | Natalie has scarcely no free time. |
| Run-on sentences | The *Brittanic* docked at West 52nd Street, a tug nosed it to its berth. |

## Spelling, capitalization, punctuation errors

These errors are self-evident. In spelling, such constructions as "alot" for "a lot" are to be considered errors. Not italicizing proper nouns and titles (or not underlining them) is an error (*Queen Elizabeth II, The New Yorker*). Punctuation errors would not include the comma splice, the run-on sentence, etc. These errors are to be classified as grammar (syntax) errors above. Misuses of the apostrophe, the dash, the semicolon, the comma, etc., are punctuation errors. As above, do not put any marks on the actual essay.

# Appendix C: Student Descriptive Questionnaire

# *Student Descriptive Questionnaire (SDQ)*

Completing the SDQ gives you a chance to send colleges information about your interests, experiences, activities, and plans, along with your test scores. Your responses may help counselors and admissions officers in advising you about your college plans. Your answers to most of the questions will appear on the score report that will be sent to you, your school, and the colleges and scholarship programs you name to receive reports. Your answers to other questions (the questionnaire identifies which ones) will *not* appear on your score reports but will be used for research and planning by educational institutions.

Mark your answers to the SDQ in item 16 of the Registration Form. You are encouraged to answer all questions, although you may omit the answer to a specific question, if you wish. Most of the questions have been written for students still in high school. If you are no longer in school, answer them as well as you can.

You can delete or change your answers at any time by using an Additional Report Request Form (see pages 13 and 14) or when you register for another test.

---

*Note:* If you have previously filled out a Student Descriptive Questionnaire and want to update your answers, record one of the following options at the beginning of the SDQ response area:

(A) Substitute my answers here for my previous answers to the same questions. Keep the other information I gave earlier.
(B) Include only my current answers. Delete all answers I gave earlier.
(C) Delete all my previous answers. I do not wish to have SDQ information in my records.

For further information on changing descriptive information, see page 14.

1. The College Board's Student Search Service is an information service for students, colleges, and governmental scholarship programs. It is free to all students who participate in the ATP and works this way:

   If you ask to participate, colleges and scholarship programs interested in students with your characteristics can ask for and receive your name, address, sex, date of birth, high school, and intended major. The answers you give to the questions that follow may be used to determine if you fit the characteristics colleges have requested in the Student Search Service. Different colleges and scholarship programs will be interested in students with specific characteristics, such as place of residence, range of test scores, intended college majors, ethnic background, and income. For example, a state scholarship program may want to identify all students within that state who are eligible for the Pell Grant program in order to notify them of when and how to apply.

   By participating, you may receive information from a variety of colleges and scholarship programs about their programs, admissions procedures, and financial aid opportunities. The mail you receive may include information from a college well known to you or come from one unfamiliar to you but with the academic program and other features you find important. In either case the Student Search Service can provide you with information you might not otherwise discover.

   Your name will be made available to the Student Search Service only if you answer "Yes" to this item.

   (Y) Yes, I want to be included in the Student Search Service.
   (N) No, I do not want to be included in the Student Search Service.

2. What kind of high school are you attending?

   (A) Public   (B) Other than public

3. Which of the following best describes your present high school program?

(A) Academic or college preparatory   (B) General
(C) Career-oriented (business, vocational, industrial arts)
(D) Other

4. About how many students are there in your high school class?

(A) Fewer than 100   (B) 100-249   (C) 250-499
(D) 500-749   (E) 750 or more

5. What is your most recent high school class rank? (For example, if you are 15th in a class of 100, you are in the second tenth.) If you do not know your rank or rank is not used in your school, give your best estimate.

(A) Highest tenth⎫           (D) Middle fifth
(B) Second tenth ⎬ top fifth  (E) Fourth fifth
(C) Second fifth              (F) Lowest fifth

Questions 6 through 11 ask you to blacken the letter corresponding to the total years of study you expect to complete in certain subject areas. Include in the total only courses you have taken since beginning the ninth grade and those you expect to complete before graduation from high school. Count less than a full year in a subject as a full year. Do not count a repeated year of the same course as an additional year of study.

(A) One year or the equivalent
(B) Two years or the equivalent
(C) Three years or the equivalent
(D) Four years or the equivalent
(E) More than four years or the equivalent
(F) I will not take any courses in the subject area.

6. English

7. Mathematics

8. Foreign Languages

9. Biological Sciences (for example, biology, botany, or zoology)

10. Physical Sciences (for example, chemistry, physics, or earth science)

11. Social Studies (for example, history, government, or geography)

For each of the subject areas in questions 12 through 17, blacken the *latest* year-end or midyear grade you received since beginning the ninth grade. For example, if you are a senior and have not taken biology or any other biological science since your sophomore year, indicate that year-end grade. If you are a junior and have completed the first half of the year in an English course, indicate that midyear grade.

   If you received the grade in an advanced, accelerated, or honors course, also blacken the letter H.

(A) Excellent (usually 90-100 or A)
(B) Good (usually 80-89 or B)
(C) Fair (usually 70-79 or C)
(D) Passing (usually 60-69 or D)
(F) Failing (usually 59 or below or F)
(G) Only "pass-fail" grades were assigned and I received a pass.
(H) The grade reported was in an advanced, accelerated, or honors course.

12. English

13. Mathematics

14. Foreign Languages

15. Biological Sciences

16. Physical Sciences

17. Social Studies

18. Will you have completed advanced high school or college-level work before entering college? If so, mark the letter for each field in which you plan to apply for advanced placement, credit-by-examination, or exemption from required courses.

(A) English              (E) Physical Sciences
(B) Mathematics          (F) Social Studies
(C) Foreign Languages    (G) Art/Music
(D) Biological Sciences

19. On the average, how many hours per week do you work in a part-time job? (Exclude vacations.)

(A) None             (E) 16 to 20 hours
(B) Less than 6 hours (F) 21 to 25 hours
(C) 6 to 10 hours    (G) 26 to 30 hours
(D) 11 to 15 hours   (H) More than 30 hours

20. How much have you participated in community or church groups while in high school?

(A) I have not been a member of any community or church group.
(B) I have belonged to one or two groups but have not participated actively.
(C) I have participated actively in one or two groups but have not held any major offices (for example, president, chairman, or treasurer).
(D) I have participated actively in more than two groups but have not held any major offices.
(E) I have participated actively and have held a major office in at least one community or church group.

21. How much have you participated in athletics in or out of high school?

(A) I have not participated in athletics.
(B) I have participated in individual or intramural athletics.
(C) I have been on one or more varsity teams but have not earned a varsity letter.
(D) I have earned one or more varsity letters in a single sport.
(E) I have earned varsity letters in more than one sport.

22. How much have you participated in clubs and organizations in high school?

(A) I have not been a member of any club or organization.
(B) I have belonged to some organizations but have not held any major offices (for example, president, editor, or class or school representative).
(C) I have held one or two major offices.
(D) I have held three or four major offices.
(E) I have held five or more major offices.

23. During your high school years how many honors or awards (for example, essay contest, debating tournament, science fair, music, art or theater competition, or membership in a scholastic honors group) have you received?

(A) None   (B) One or two   (C) Three or four
(D) Five or six   (E) Seven or more

24. What is the highest level of education you plan to complete beyond high school?
    (A) A two-year specialized training program (for example, electronics or laboratory technician)
    (B) A two-year Associate of Arts degree (A.A.)
    (C) Bachelor's degree (B.A. or B.S.)
    (D) Master's degree (M.A. or M.S.)
    (E) Doctor's or other professional degree (such as M.D. or Ph.D.)
    (F) Other or undecided

25. What is the date of your high school graduation? Blacken month and last two digits of year.

26. When do you expect to enter college? Blacken month and last two digits of year.

Your response to question 27 will not be included in the reports that are sent to you, your school, and the colleges you designate.

27. Do you plan to apply for financial aid at any college?
    (Y) Yes  (N) No

28. When you enroll, do you expect to attend college
    (A) full-time  (B) part-time

29. When you enroll, do you expect to attend college during the
    (A) day  (B) evening

30. Where do you prefer to live during your first two years in college?
    (A) At home
    (B) Single-sex dorm
    (C) Coed dorm
    (D) Fraternity or sorority house
    (E) On-campus apartment
    (F) Off-campus apartment

31. Are you a United States citizen?
    (Y) Yes  (N) No

32. Are you a veteran of the United States Armed Forces?
    (Y) Yes  (N) No

Questions 33 through 36 are for students who have finished high school and have already attended college. If you have not, go on to the paragraph preceding question 37.

33. Please put the code number of the college you are attending or most recently attended in the spaces provided and blacken the corresponding ovals. See the gray-bordered pages for college code numbers.

34. Are you enrolled in that college now?
    (Y) Yes  (N) No

35. Approximately what was your grade point average at that college on a scale of 0 (F) to 4 (A)?
    (A) 3.5 or above
    (B) 3.0–3.4
    (C) 2.5–2.9
    (D) 2.0–2.4
    (E) 1.5–1.9
    (F) Below 1.5
    (G) Not applicable

36. If you expect to transfer credits, at what level do you expect to enter the new college?
    (A) First semester freshman
    (B) Second semester freshman
    (C) First semester sophomore
    (D) Second semester sophomore
    (E) Junior
    (F) Senior

The College Board wants its tests and services to be fair and useful to all candidates. Research based on responses to questions 37 and 38 will help the College Board evaluate and improve its tests and services. Your responses will also be reported to your school and to those colleges that accept such information in order to make sure their programs are fair and useful to students of all racial and ethnic backgrounds.

37. How do you describe yourself?
    (A) American Indian or Alaskan native
    (B) Black or Afro-American or Negro
    (C) Mexican-American or Chicano
    (D) Oriental or Asian-American or Pacific Islander
    (E) Puerto Rican
    (F) White or Caucasian
    (G) Other

38. Is English your best language?
    (Y) Yes  (N) No

Your responses to questions 39 and 40 will be used only for research. They will not be included in the score reports that are sent to you, your school, and the colleges you designate.

39. Indicate the highest level of education completed by your father or male guardian.
    (A) Grade school
    (B) Some high school
    (C) High school diploma
    (D) Business or trade school
    (E) Some college
    (F) Bachelor's degree
    (G) Some graduate or professional school
    (H) Graduate or professional degree

40. Using the list in question 39, indicate the highest level of education completed by your mother or female guardian.

Questions 41 through 43 ask about your parents' financial situation and should be answered in consultation with them. Your individual responses will not be reported to anyone. Only summary responses for groups of students will be reported to colleges and high schools.

41. How many persons are dependent on your parent(s) or legal guardian for financial support? Be sure to include your parent(s) and yourself.
    (A) Two  (B) Three  (C) Four  (D) Five
    (E) Six  (F) Seven  (G) Eight  (H) Nine or more

42. During your first year in college, how many persons dependent on your parent(s) or legal guardian will be in college? Include yourself.
    (A) One  (B) Two  (C) Three
    (D) Four  (E) Five or more

43. What was the approximate income of your parents before taxes last year? Include taxable and nontaxable income from all sources.

(A) Less than $3,000 a year (about $57 a week or less)
(B) Between $3,000 and $5,999 a year (from $58 to $114 a week)
(C) Between $6,000 and $8,999 a year (from $115 to $173 a week)
(D) Between $9,000 and $11,999 a year (from $174 to $230 a week)
(E) Between $12,000 and $14,999 a year (from $231 to $288 a week)
(F) Between $15,000 and $17,999 a year (from $289 to $346 a week)
(G) Between $18,000 and $20,999 a year (from $347 to $403 a week)
(H) Between $21,000 and $23,999 a year
(I) Between $24,000 and $26,999 a year
(J) Between $27,000 and $29,999 a year
(K) Between $30,000 and $34,999 a year
(L) Between $35,000 and $39,999 a year
(M) Between $40,000 and $44,999 a year
(N) Between $45,000 and $49,000 a year
(O) $50,000 a year or more

44. You may want to receive help outside regular course work from the college you plan to attend. If so, blacken the letter for each area in which you may want help.

(A) Counseling about educational plans and opportunities
(B) Counseling about vocational/career plans and opportunities
(C) Improving mathematical ability
(D) Finding part-time work
(E) Counseling about personal problems
(F) Increasing reading ability
(G) Developing good study habits
(H) Improving writing ability

Questions 45 and 46 concern your interests in extracurricular activities in high school and your plans to participate in college.

45. Blacken the letter for each activity in which you participated while in high school.

(A) Athletics—interscholastic, intramural, or community
(B) Ethnic or racial activities or organizations
(C) Journalism, debating, or dramatic activities
(D) Art, music, or dance
(E) Preprofessional or departmental clubs—for example, Future Teachers of America, American Society of Civil Engineers
(F) Religious activities or organizations
(G) Social clubs or community organizations
(H) Student government

46. Using the list in question 45, blacken the letter for each activity in which you plan to participate in college.

Questions 47 through 60 concern how you feel you compare with other people your own age in certain areas of ability. For each field, blacken the letter

(A) if you feel you are in the highest 1 percent in that area of ability
(B) if you feel you are in the highest 10 percent in that area of ability
(C) if you feel you are above average in that area of ability
(D) if you feel you are average in that area of ability
(E) if you feel you are below average in that area of ability

47. Acting ability

48. Artistic ability

49. Athletic ability

50. Creative writing

51. Getting along with others

52. Leadership ability

53. Mathematical ability

54. Mechanical ability

55. Musical ability

56. Organizing work

57. Sales ability

58. Scientific ability

59. Spoken expression

60. Written expression

61. From the list on page 10, choose the field that would be your first choice for your college curriculum. Write the number of that field and blacken the corresponding ovals.

62. From the same list, choose the field that would be your second choice. Write the number of that field and blacken the corresponding ovals.

63. From the same list, choose the career field that you think you will pursue after college. Write the number of that field and blacken the corresponding ovals. If your exact choice does not appear, select the one most closely related.

The 1984–85 Student Descriptive Questionnaire is printed by permission of Educational Testing Service, the copyright owner.

## Appendix D: Instructor's rating form and instructions

*Instructor's grade and rating sheet*

Institution: _____  Class: _____

| ID | Student name | Course grade | Writing skill ratings* | |
|----|--------------|--------------|------------------------|--------------|
| | | | Discourse | Mechanics |
| 117 | | _____ | _____ | _____ |
| 118 | | _____ | _____ | _____ |
| 119 | | _____ | _____ | _____ |
| 120 | | _____ | _____ | _____ |
| 121 | | _____ | _____ | _____ |
| 122 | | _____ | _____ | _____ |
| 123 | | _____ | _____ | _____ |
| 124 | | _____ | _____ | _____ |
| 125 | | _____ | _____ | _____ |
| 126 | | _____ | _____ | _____ |
| 127 | | _____ | _____ | _____ |
| 128 | | _____ | _____ | _____ |
| 129 | | _____ | _____ | _____ |
| 130 | | _____ | _____ | _____ |
| 131 | | _____ | _____ | _____ |
| 132 | | _____ | _____ | _____ |
| 133 | | _____ | _____ | _____ |
| 134 | | _____ | _____ | _____ |
| 135 | | _____ | _____ | _____ |
| 136 | | _____ | _____ | _____ |
| 137 | | _____ | _____ | _____ |

* See attached instructions for an explanation of these ratings.

# Instructions for instructor's grade and rating sheet

This grade and rating sheet is an essential component of the second measurement-of-writing-ability project. Grades and ratings will be compared with other information collected in the project. The ratings are important because course grades often represent many factors, and one objective in the MWA 2 project is to isolate specific student strengths and weaknesses where possible. If a student transferred out of your class section to another class section during the course of the term, please note that. Please do not attempt the ratings for students who withdrew or who received incomplete grades. Your best judgment on the ratings will be greatly appreciated.

## Course grade

It is assumed that all participating institutions use standard grading procedures, but that there may be variations. Enter the grade that a student actually received in the course. If there is something unusual about the grading system, please explain. If " +'s" and " −'s" are used, please include them in the course grade.

## Discourse rating

Using your standard grading procedures, assign to the student a "grade" that represents your best judgment of that student's overall ability in written discourse. The term *discourse* is intended to include English composition ability generally: the ability to organize thoughts, use appropriate rhetorical strategies, use supporting material when needed, develop a thesis, generate noteworthy ideas, make effective transitions, maintain coherence and unity, etc. If the only consideration in assigning course grades is a student's writing ability, the grade assigned for the discourse rating may be the same as the course grade. One would normally expect, however, that a course grade represents more than a skill. Completion of assignments properly and on time and class participation, for example, may influence the course grade, but they should not influence your judgments of a student's writing skill.

## Mechanics rating

Using your standard grading procedures, assign to the student a "grade" that represents your best judgment of that student's mastery of English composition mechanics. The term *mechanics* is intended to include sentence-level skills such as those that enable a student to avoid errors in subject-verb agreement, tense, verb form, connectives, logical comparisons, modifiers, pronouns, diction, idiom, parallelism, sentence fragments, punctuation, subordination, coordination, etc. An A student may still have problems with mechanics and, therefore, may receive a mechanics rating less than A. A student with a course grade of C may have reasonably good skills in mechanics but still not be able to write well. Accordingly, a student may be assigned an A in mechanics but a lower rating in discourse.

# Appendix E: Technical notes

1. Course grades were assigned on a scale from A to F, with + and − grades included. One institution did not use + and − grades, and it was observed additionally that the grades in that institution were relatively lower than the grades in the five other institutions compared with writing performance. Since it was believed that the grading scale was substantially different for this institution, its grades were adjusted to bring the grade average in line with the student writing performance average in that institution. Consideration was also given to a pooled, within group, correlational approach as a means of handling the problem of varying grading standards across institutions. Experiments with this approach (standardizing grades within institution) showed that it attenuated relationships with grades because institutional grades generally correlated reasonably well with writing performance.

2. Not all students with complete essay data had complete data on all other variables. The ECT data were missing for 57 of these students either because the participating institution did not require the ECT for admissions or because no special ECT administration was conducted.

3. There were two complications in this sample. One complication was that several different ECT forms were involved, and one of the forms was a retired form used for special ECT administrations in two institutions that did not require the ECT. This retired form could be equated with regular administration forms only through approximate methods. A second complication was that some of the regular administration forms were short forms designed to be combined with essay scores from December administrations of the ECT. Thus, the ECT scores for December administrations include an essay score as a component. Since we wanted to compare the multiple-choice ECT scores with the essay scores of this study, a statistical procedure was used to remove the essay scores from the December ECT scores.

4. Even though no adjustments were made for the essay components of some ECT scores in this sample, correlational results did not appear to have been affected in any observable sense. For example, average ECT correlations with writing performance (see Table 6.5) were about the same in Sample B (.61) as in Sample C (.62).

5. Despite the use of all multiple-choice ECT scores in this sample, the average correlation of ECT scores with later writing performance (see Table 6.5) was greater for this sample than for the other samples (.66). An additional indication that Sample D ECT data may be superior to the ECT data of Samples B and C is the correlation between ECT scores and TSWE scores in this sample (.87).

6. The Spearman-Brown formula, intended primarily for estimating the effect that lengthening a test has on reliability, can also be used to estimate the effects of number of readers and numbers of essays:

$$r_{nn} = \frac{nr_{tt}}{1 + (n - 1)r_{tt}}$$

where
$r_{nn}$ = estimated reliability for a longer test
$r_{tt}$ = estimated reliability for the present test
$n$ = number of times the test is lengthened

In essay assessments, for example, using two readings instead of one reading is considered a doubling of test length.

7. The possibility that the correlational differences between Samples A and D might be due to restriction of range was examined using the following correction formula for Cohen and Cohen (1975):

$$\bar{r} = \frac{r^* (\sigma/\sigma^*)}{\sqrt{1 - r^{*2} + r^{*2} (\sigma^2/\sigma^{*2})}}$$

where
$\bar{r}$ = corrected correlation coefficient
$r^*$ = observed correlation coefficient
$\sigma$ = population standard deviation
$\sigma^*$ = sample standard deviation

Both Sample A and Sample D correlations between TSWE and total essay score were corrected to the correlation that would be expected in the national sample.

Sample A: $\bar{r}$ = .74

Sample D: $\bar{r}$ = .78

8. The comparisons here are for composite scores made up of a 60-minute multiple-choice test and a 45-minute or longer essay test. In the Admissions Testing Program of the College Board, the ECT contains—for some administrations—a 20-minute essay. In those administrations, the multiple-choice portion of the ECT is reduced to 40 minutes to leave 20 minutes for the essay. For a composite score based on such shorter tests, lower validities would be expected.

**Appendix F: Tables**

## Table F.1. Descriptions of major variables, Sample A

| Label | Mean | Standard deviation | Minimum value | Maximum value | N | Abbreviation |
|---|---|---|---|---|---|---|
| SAT-V | 443.479 | 84.808 | 200 | 730 | 267 | SATV |
| SAT-M | 506.348 | 100.345 | 235 | 710 | 267 | SATM |
| SAT-reading | 44.745 | 8.860 | 20 | 68 | 267 | SATR |
| SAT-vocabulary | 44.375 | 9.042 | 20 | 77 | 267 | SATVOC |
| TSWE | 45.427 | 8.034 | 20 | 60 | 267 | TSWE |
| Course grade | 8.573 | 1.986 | 3 | 14 | 267 | COURSE |
| Discourse skills | 8.337 | 1.975 | 3 | 14 | 267 | DISC |
| Mechanics | 8.142 | 2.257 | 1 | 14 | 267 | MECH |
| Writing skill | 16.479 | 3.747 | 7.00 | 25.00 | 267 | WRSKILL |
| Narrative 1 | 11.225 | 2.663 | 3.00 | 18.00 | 267 | NAR1 |
| Narrative 2 | 11.371 | 2.887 | 3.00 | 18.00 | 267 | NAR2 |
| Expository 1 | 10.899 | 2.761 | 3.00 | 18.00 | 267 | EXP1 |
| Expository 2 | 10.828 | 2.724 | 3.00 | 18.00 | 267 | EXP2 |
| Persuasive 1 | 11.442 | 3.218 | 3.00 | 18.00 | 267 | PER1 |
| Persuasive 2 | 11.974 | 3.050 | 3.00 | 18.00 | 267 | PER2 |
| Narrative total | 22.596 | 4.893 | 7.00 | 36.00 | 267 | NARTOTAL |
| Expository total | 21.727 | 4.865 | 7.00 | 36.00 | 267 | EXPTOTAL |
| Persuasive total | 23.416 | 5.676 | 7.00 | 36.00 | 267 | PERTOTAL |
| Narrative + expository | 44.322 | 8.969 | 17.00 | 67.00 | 267 | NOTPER |
| Narrative + persuasive | 46.011 | 9.173 | 20.00 | 68.00 | 267 | NOTEXP |
| Persuasive + expository | 45.142 | 9.347 | 20.00 | 68.00 | 267 | NOTNAR |
| Holistic total | 67.738 | 13.120 | 32.00 | 101.00 | 267 | ESSAY |

## Table F.2. Descriptions of major variables, Sample B

| Label | Mean | Standard deviation | Minimum value | Maximum value | N | Abbreviation |
|---|---|---|---|---|---|---|
| SAT-V | 446.800 | 87.368 | 220 | 730 | 210 | SATV |
| SAT-M | 501.790 | 101.536 | 280 | 710 | 210 | SATM |
| SAT-reading | 45.048 | 9.147 | 21 | 68 | 210 | SATR |
| SAT-vocabulary | 44.710 | 9.234 | 20 | 77 | 210 | SATVOC |
| TSWE | 45.748 | 7.983 | 20 | 60 | 210 | TSWE |
| ECT | 450.762 | 78.032 | 270.00 | 660.00 | 210 | ECT |
| Course grade | 8.590 | 2.006 | 3 | 14 | 210 | COURSE |
| Discourse skills | 8.338 | 1.960 | 3 | 14 | 210 | DISC |
| Mechanics | 8.248 | 2.264 | 1 | 14 | 210 | MECH |
| Writing skill | 16.586 | 3.812 | 7.00 | 25.00 | 210 | WRSKILL |
| Narrative 1 | 11.333 | 2.712 | 3.00 | 18.00 | 210 | NAR1 |
| Narrative 2 | 11.443 | 2.794 | 3.00 | 18.00 | 210 | NAR2 |
| Expository 1 | 11.029 | 2.634 | 3.00 | 18.00 | 210 | EXP1 |
| Expository 2 | 11.095 | 2.588 | 3.00 | 18.00 | 210 | EXP2 |
| Persuasive 1 | 11.462 | 3.245 | 3.00 | 18.00 | 210 | PER1 |
| Persuasive 2 | 12.010 | 3.061 | 3.00 | 18.00 | 210 | PER2 |
| Narrative total | 22.776 | 4.864 | 7.00 | 36.00 | 210 | NARTOTAL |
| Expository total | 22.124 | 4.678 | 7.00 | 36.00 | 210 | EXPTOTAL |
| Persuasive total | 23.471 | 5.748 | 7.00 | 36.00 | 210 | PERTOTAL |
| Narrative + expository | 44.900 | 8.791 | 17.00 | 67.00 | 210 | NOTPER |
| Narrative + persuasive | 46.248 | 9.164 | 20.00 | 68.00 | 210 | NOTEXP |
| Persuasive + expository | 45.595 | 9.292 | 20.00 | 68.00 | 210 | NOTNAR |
| Holistic total | 60.971 | 13.001 | 32.00 | 101.00 | 210 | ESSAY |

## Table F.3. Descriptions of major variables, Sample C

| Label | Mean | Standard deviation | Minimum value | Maximum value | N | Abbreviation |
|---|---|---|---|---|---|---|
| SAT-V | 459.298 | 81.469 | 225 | 730 | 141 | SATV |
| SAT-M | 529.270 | 95.268 | 235 | 710 | 141 | SATM |
| SAT-reading | 46.305 | 8.666 | 21 | 68 | 141 | SATR |
| SAT-vocabulary | 45.865 | 8.679 | 20 | 77 | 141 | SATVOC |
| TSWE | 47.021 | 7.913 | 20 | 60 | 141 | TSWE |
| ECT | 470.567 | 76.607 | 270 | 660 | 141 | ECT |
| Course grade | 8.816 | 1.973 | 4 | 14 | 141 | COURSE |
| Discourse skills | 8.518 | 2.093 | 3 | 14 | 141 | DISC |
| Mechanics | 8.582 | 2.129 | 3 | 14 | 141 | MECH |
| Writing skill | 17.099 | 3.737 | 9.00 | 25.00 | 141 | WRSKILL |
| Narrative 1 | 11.624 | 2.804 | 3.00 | 18.00 | 141 | NAR1 |
| Narrative 2 | 11.716 | 2.931 | 3.00 | 18.00 | 141 | NAR2 |
| Expository 1 | 11.433 | 2.681 | 3.00 | 18.00 | 141 | EXP1 |
| Expository 2 | 11.525 | 2.568 | 4.00 | 18.00 | 141 | EXP2 |
| Persuasive 1 | 12.383 | 2.978 | 5.00 | 18.00 | 141 | PER1 |
| Persuasive 2 | 12.759 | 2.764 | 3.00 | 18.00 | 141 | PER2 |
| Narrative total | 23.340 | 5.074 | 7.00 | 35.00 | 141 | NARTOTAL |
| Expository total | 22.957 | 4.757 | 7.00 | 36.00 | 141 | EXPTOTAL |
| Persuasive total | 25.142 | 5.212 | 11.00 | 36.00 | 141 | PERTOTAL |
| Narrative + expository | 46.298 | 9.097 | 17.00 | 67.00 | 141 | NOTPER |
| Narrative + persuasive | 48.482 | 9.049 | 20.00 | 68.00 | 141 | NOTEXP |
| Persuasive + expository | 48.099 | 8.854 | 21.00 | 68.00 | 141 | NOTNAR |
| Holistic total | 71.440 | 12.942 | 33.00 | 101.00 | 141 | ESSAY |

# Table F.4. Descriptions of major variables, Sample D

| Label | Mean | Standard deviation | Minimum value | Maximum value | N | Abbreviation |
|---|---|---|---|---|---|---|
| SAT-V | 462.128 | 88.664 | 225 | 730 | 94 | SATV |
| SAT-M | 524.660 | 94.115 | 310 | 710 | 94 | SATM |
| SAT-reading | 46.660 | 9.506 | 21 | 68 | 94 | SATR |
| SAT-vocabulary | 46.064 | 9.368 | 20 | 77 | 94 | SATVOC |
| TSWE | 46.628 | 8.752 | 20 | 60 | 94 | TSWE |
| ECT | 466.809 | 80.475 | 270 | 660 | 94 | ECT |
| Course grade | 8.755 | 1.876 | 5 | 14 | 94 | COURSE |
| Discourse skills | 8.426 | 1.948 | 3 | 14 | 94 | DISC |
| Mechanics | 8.426 | 2.128 | 3 | 14 | 94 | MECH |
| Writing skill | 16.851 | 3.522 | 9.00 | 25.00 | 94 | WRSKILL |
| Narrative 1 | 11.543 | 2.880 | 3.00 | 18.00 | 94 | NAR1 |
| Narrative 2 | 11.638 | 2.962 | 3.00 | 18.00 | 94 | NAR2 |
| Expository 1 | 11.351 | 2.902 | 3.00 | 18.00 | 94 | EXP1 |
| Expository 2 | 11.362 | 2.444 | 4.00 | 18.00 | 94 | EXP2 |
| Persuasive 1 | 12.266 | 2.908 | 6.00 | 18.00 | 94 | PER1 |
| Persuasive 2 | 12.489 | 2.479 | 3.00 | 17.00 | 94 | PER2 |
| Narrative total | 23.181 | 5.199 | 7.00 | 34.00 | 94 | NARTOTAL |
| Expository total | 22.713 | 4.916 | 7.00 | 36.00 | 94 | EXPTOTAL |
| Persuasive total | 24.755 | 4.959 | 11.00 | 35.00 | 94 | PERTOTAL |
| Narrative + expository | 45.894 | 9.362 | 17.00 | 67.00 | 94 | NOTPER |
| Narrative + persuasive | 47.936 | 8.895 | 20.00 | 68.00 | 94 | NOTEXP |
| Persuasive + expository | 47.468 | 8.825 | 21.00 | 68.00 | 94 | NOTNAR |
| Holistic total | 70.649 | 12.994 | 33.00 | 101.00 | 94 | ESSAY |
| Total words written | 3110.319 | 748.118 | 1532.00 | 5966.00 | 94 | WORDS |
| GUSS error count/1,000 words | 26.436 | 11.785 | 7.15 | 70.73 | 94 | R12ABC |
| PSC error count/1,000 words | 25.527 | 13.815 | 5.11 | 90.76 | 94 | R12DEF |
| Total error count/1,000 words | 51.963 | 22.675 | 12.26 | 141.09 | 94 | R12TOT |

*Table F.5. Correlations of major variables, Sample A*

| | SATV | SATM | SATR | SATVOC | TSWE | COURSE | DISC | MECH | WRSKILL | NAR1 | NAR2 |
|---|---|---|---|---|---|---|---|---|---|---|---|
| SATV | 1.0000 | .5599** | .9457** | .9435** | .6981** | .4423** | .3567** | .4444** | .4557** | .5001** | .3836** |
| SATM | .5599** | 1.0000 | .5276** | .5307** | .4573** | .2004** | .1705* | .1984** | .2094** | .3012** | .1572* |
| SATR | .9457** | .5276** | 1.0000 | .7911** | .6617** | .4264** | .3379** | .4238** | .4333** | .4787** | .3648** |
| SATVOC | .9435** | .5307** | .7911** | 1.0000 | .6620** | .4178** | .3436** | .4141** | .4305** | .4696** | .3489** |
| TSWE | .6981** | .4573** | .6617** | .6620** | 1.0000 | .4066** | .2979** | .5285** | .4753** | .5729** | .4592** |
| COURSE | .4423** | .2004** | .4264** | .4178** | .4066** | 1.0000 | .8552** | .6964** | .8702** | .4418** | .4376** |
| DISC | .3567** | .1705* | .3379** | .3436** | .2979** | .8552** | 1.0000 | .5661** | .8681** | .3322** | .3901** |
| MECH | .4444** | .1984** | .4238** | .4141** | .5285** | .6964** | .5661** | 1.0000 | .9007** | .4701** | .4772** |
| WRSKILL | .4557** | .2094** | .4333** | .4305** | .4753** | .8702** | .8681** | .9007** | 1.0000 | .4582** | .4931** |
| NAR1 | .5001** | .3012** | .4787** | .4696** | .5729** | .4418** | .3322** | .4701** | .4582** | 1.0000 | .5540** |
| NAR2 | .3836** | .1572* | .3648** | .3489** | .4592** | .4376** | .3901** | .4772** | .4931** | .5540** | 1.0000 |
| EXP1 | .4657** | .2304** | .4383** | .4254** | .5090** | .3766** | .3144** | .4071** | .4109** | .5332** | .6004** |
| EXP2 | .4210** | .2668** | .4142** | .3828** | .4489** | .4366** | .3392** | .5012** | .4806** | .5132** | .5068** |
| PER1 | .3899** | .2950** | .3782** | .3568** | .4825** | .5226** | .4095** | .5800** | .5652** | .4302** | .3948** |
| PER2 | .3411** | .1969** | .3371** | .3042** | .3978** | .5020** | .4277** | .5309** | .5452** | .3668** | .4157** |
| NARTOTAL | .4985** | .2567** | .4757** | .4614** | .5827** | .4986** | .4110** | .5374** | .5403** | .8711** | .8914** |
| EXPTOTAL | .5001** | .2802** | .4807** | .4558** | .5403** | .4583** | .3684** | .5118** | .5024** | .5901** | .6246** |
| PERTOTAL | .4044** | .2731** | .3956** | .3657** | .4873** | .5661** | .4620** | .6141** | .6134** | .4410** | .4472** |
| NOTPER | .5432** | .2920** | .5203** | .4990** | .6110** | .5206** | .4240** | .5708** | .5673** | .7953** | .8251** |
| NOTEXP | .5161** | .3059** | .4985** | .4724** | .6124** | .6162** | .5051** | .6666** | .6677** | .7375** | .7522** |
| NOTNAR | .5058** | .3116** | .4904** | .4593** | .5771** | .5822** | .4723** | .6392** | .6339** | .5749** | .5966** |
| ESSAY | .5463** | .3177** | .5268** | .4993** | .6285** | .6008** | .4897** | .6558** | .6531** | .7344** | .7575** |

Table F.5. continued

| | EXP1 | EXP2 | PER1 | PER2 | NARTOTAL | EXPTOTAL | PERTOTAL | NOTPER | NOTEXP | NOTNAR | ESSAY |
|---|---|---|---|---|---|---|---|---|---|---|---|
| SATV | .4657** | .4210** | .3899* | .3411** | .4985** | .5001** | .4044** | .5437** | .5161** | .5058** | .5463** |
| SATM | .2304*** | .2668*** | .2950*** | .1969** | .2567** | .2802** | .2731** | .2920** | .3059*** | .3116*** | .3177*** |
| SATR | .4383*** | .4142*** | .3782*** | .3371** | .4757** | .4807** | .3956** | .5203** | .4985** | .4904** | .5268** |
| SATVOC | .4254*** | .3823*** | .3568*** | .3042** | .4614** | .4558** | .3657** | .4990** | .4724** | .4593** | .4993** |
| TSWE | .5090*** | .4489*** | .4825*** | .3978** | .5827** | .5403** | .4873** | .6110** | .6124** | .5771** | .6285** |
| COURSE | .3766*** | .4366*** | .5226*** | .5020** | .4986** | .4583** | .5661** | .5206** | .6162** | .5822** | .6008** |
| DISC | .3144*** | .3392*** | .4095*** | .4277** | .4110** | .3684** | .4620** | .4240** | .5051** | .4723** | .4897** |
| MECH | .4071*** | .5012*** | .5800*** | .5309** | .5374** | .5118** | .6141** | .5708** | .6666** | .6392** | .6558** |
| WRSKILL | .4109*** | .4806*** | .5652*** | .5452** | .5403** | .5024** | .6134** | .5673** | .6677** | .6339** | .6531** |
| NAR1 | .5332*** | .5132*** | .4302*** | .3668** | .8711** | .5901** | .4410** | .7953** | .7375** | .5749** | .7344** |
| NAR2 | .6004*** | .5068*** | .3948*** | .4157** | .8914** | .6246** | .4472** | .8251** | .7522** | .5966** | .7575** |
| EXP1 | 1.0000 | .5729*** | .4324*** | .4224** | .6444** | .8884** | .4721** | .8335** | .6359** | .7491** | .7740** |
| EXP2 | .5729*** | 1.0000 | .5152*** | .4609** | .5783** | .8852** | .5398** | .7956** | .6425** | .7885** | .7774** |
| PER1 | .4324*** | .5152*** | 1.0000 | .6397** | .4670** | .5340** | .9107** | .5444** | .8126** | .8309** | .7661** |
| PER2 | .4224*** | .4609** | .6397** | 1.0000 | .4449** | .4979** | .9001** | .5128** | .7942** | .8056** | .7399** |
| NARTOTAL | .6444*** | .5783** | .4670** | .4449** | 1.0000 | .6896** | .5038** | .9196** | .8452** | .6649** | .8466** |
| EXPTOTAL | .8884*** | .8852** | .5340** | .4979** | .6896** | 1.0000 | .5703** | .9187** | .7207** | .8667** | .8747** |
| PERTOTAL | .4721*** | .5398** | .9107** | .9001** | .5038** | .5703** | 1.0000 | .5842** | .8875** | .9040** | .8320** |
| NOTPER | .8335** | .7956** | .5444** | .5128** | .9196** | .9187** | .5842** | 1.0000 | .8520** | .8328** | .9363** |
| NOTEXP | .6359** | .6425** | .8126** | .7942** | .8452** | .7207** | .8875** | .8520** | 1.0000 | .9140** | .9664** |
| NOTNAR | .7491** | .7885** | .8309** | .8056** | .6649** | .8667** | .9040** | .8328** | .9140** | 1.0000 | .9604** |
| ESSAY | .7740** | .7774** | .7661** | .7399** | .8466** | .8747** | .8320** | .9363** | .9664** | .9604** | 1.0000 |

* signif. ≤ .01.
** signif. ≤ .001.

*Table F.6. Correlations of major variables, Sample B*

| | SATV | SATM | SATR | SATVOC | TSWE | ECT | COURSE | DISC | MECH | WRSKILL | NAR1 |
|---|---|---|---|---|---|---|---|---|---|---|---|
| SATV | 1.0000 | .6081** | .9487** | .9456** | .6957** | .6808** | .4835** | .3919** | .4510** | .4694** | .4879** |
| SATM | .6081** | 1.0000 | .5680** | .5804** | .5480** | .5188** | .2763** | .2221** | .2770** | .2787** | .3227** |
| SATR | .9487** | .5680** | 1.0000 | .8007** | .6558** | .6463** | .4703** | .3730** | .4294** | .4468** | .4747** |
| SATVOC | .9456** | .5804** | .8007** | 1.0000 | .6690** | .6438** | .4516** | .3729** | .4212** | .4419** | .4510** |
| TSWE | .6957** | .5480** | .6558** | .6690** | 1.0000 | .8079** | .4459** | .3531** | .5139** | .4868** | .5640** |
| ECT | .6808** | .5188** | .6463** | .6438** | .8079** | 1.0000 | .4449** | .3665** | .5317** | .5043** | .5549** |
| COURSE | .4835** | .2763** | .4703** | .4516** | .4459** | .4449** | 1.0000 | .8630** | .7295** | .8770** | .4642** |
| DISC | .3919** | .2221** | .3730** | .3729** | .3531** | .3665** | .8630** | 1.0000 | .6269** | .8865** | .3748** |
| MECH | .4510** | .2770** | .4294** | .4212** | .5139** | .5317** | .7295** | .6269** | 1.0000 | .9162** | .4394** |
| WRSKILL | .4694** | .2787** | .4468** | .4419** | .4868** | .5043** | .8770** | .8865** | .9162** | 1.0000 | .4536** |
| NAR1 | .4879** | .3227** | .4747** | .4510** | .5640** | .5549** | .4642** | .3748** | .4394** | .4536** | 1.0000 |
| NAR2 | .3583** | .2176** | .3476** | .3141** | .4319** | .3813** | .4705** | .4329** | .4357** | .4813** | .5608** |
| EXP1 | .4488** | .2992** | .4230** | .4093** | .5299** | .4575** | .4334** | .3698** | .4209** | .4401** | .5601** |
| EXP2 | .4377** | .3090** | .4285** | .3987** | .4916** | .4675** | .5043** | .4303** | .5161** | .5278** | .5259** |
| PER1 | .4080** | .3633** | .3452** | .3723** | .4957** | .5221** | .5490** | .4350** | .5908** | .5746** | .4273** |
| PER2 | .3478** | .2487** | .3476** | .2999** | .3966** | .4054** | .4839** | .4134** | .5231** | .5232** | .3726** |
| NARTOTAL | .4778** | .3049** | .4643** | .4319** | .5625** | .5284** | .5291** | .4576** | .4952** | .5294** | .8796** |
| EXPTOTAL | .4949** | .3394** | .4753** | .4511** | .5704** | .5163** | .5231** | .4463** | .5226** | .5398** | .6064** |
| PERTOTAL | .4156** | .3375** | .4082** | .3699** | .4910** | .5106** | .5676** | .4657** | .6121** | .6030** | .4396** |
| NOTPER | .5277** | .3493** | .5098** | .4790** | .6148** | .5671** | .5711** | .4907** | .5521** | .5802** | .8093** |
| NOTEXP | .5142** | .3735** | .5024** | .4612** | .6065** | .6007** | .6368** | .5350** | .6467** | .6591** | .7426** |
| NOTNAR | .5062** | .3146** | .4918** | .4559** | .5909** | .5757** | .6144** | .5127** | .6417** | .6447** | .5772** |
| ESSAY | .5405** | .3854** | .5252** | .4874** | .6328** | .6092** | .6371** | .5377** | .6439** | .6588** | .7416** |

Table F.6. continued

| | NAR2 | EXP1 | EXP2 | PER1 | PER2 | NARTOTAL | EXPTOTAL | PERTOTAL | NOTPER | NOTEXP | NOTNAR | ESSAY |
|---|---|---|---|---|---|---|---|---|---|---|---|---|
| SATV | .3583** | .4488** | .4377** | .4080** | .3478** | .4778** | .4949** | .4156** | .5277** | .5142** | .5062** | .5405** |
| SATM | .2176** | .2992** | .3090** | .3633** | .2487** | .3049** | .3394** | .3375** | .3493** | .3735** | .3796** | .3854** |
| SATR | .3476** | .4230** | .4285** | .3952** | .3476** | .4543** | .4753** | .4082** | .5098** | .5024** | .4918** | .5252** |
| SATVOC | .3141** | .4093** | .3987** | .3723** | .2999** | .4319** | .4511** | .3699** | .4790** | .4612** | .4559** | .4874** |
| TSWE | .4319** | .5299** | .4916** | .4957** | .3966** | .5525** | .5704** | .4910** | .6148** | .6065** | .5909** | .6328** |
| ECT | .3813** | .4575** | .4675** | .5221** | .4054** | .5384** | .5163** | .5106** | .5671** | .6007** | .5757** | .6092** |
| COURSE | .4705** | .4334** | .5043** | .5490** | .4639** | .5291** | .5231** | .5676** | .5711** | .6368** | .6144** | .6371** |
| DISC | .4329** | .3698** | .4303** | .4350** | .4134** | .4576** | .4463** | .4657** | .4907** | .5350** | .5127** | .5377** |
| MECH | .4357** | .4209** | .5161** | .5908** | .5231** | .5294** | .5226** | .6121** | .5521** | .6467** | .6417** | .6439** |
| WRSKILL | .4813** | .4401** | .5278** | .5746** | .5232** | .5294** | .5398** | .6030** | .5802** | .6591** | .6447** | .6588** |
| NAR1 | .5608** | .5601** | .5259** | .4273** | .3726** | .8296** | .6064** | .4396** | .8093** | .7426** | .5772** | .7416** |
| NAR2 | 1.0000 | .5860** | .5347** | .3689** | .4034** | .8671** | .6258** | .4231** | .8238** | .7362** | .5767** | .7441** |
| EXP1 | .5860** | 1.0000 | .6046** | .4553** | .4582** | .6139** | .8976** | .5010** | .8367** | .6586** | .7618** | .7872** |
| EXP2 | .5347** | .6046** | 1.0000 | .5292** | .4649** | .6003** | .8938** | .5463** | .8077** | .6612** | .7879** | .7877** |
| PER1 | .3689** | .4553** | .5292** | 1.0000 | .6615** | .4521** | .5492** | .9168** | .5413** | .8139** | .8436** | .7713** |
| PER2 | .4034** | .4582** | .4649** | .6615** | 1.0000 | .4335** | .5153** | .9060** | .5173** | .8015** | .8198** | .7503** |
| NARTOTAL | .8871** | .6489** | .6003** | .4501** | .4395** | 1.0000 | .6975** | .4881** | .9245** | .8369** | .6531** | .8409** |
| EXPTOTAL | .6258** | .8976** | .8938** | .5492** | .5153** | .6975** | 1.0000 | .5844** | .9181** | .7367** | .8649** | .8791** |
| PERTOTAL | .4231** | .5010** | .5463** | .9168** | .9060** | .4881** | .5844** | 1.0000 | .5811** | .8862** | .9128** | .8350** |
| NOTPER | .8238** | .8367** | .8077** | .5413** | .5173** | .9245** | .9181** | .5811** | 1.0000 | .8551** | .8216** | .9330** |
| NOTEXP | .7362** | .6586** | .6612** | .8139** | .8015** | .8369** | .7367** | .8862** | .8551** | 1.0000 | .9191** | .9700** |
| NOTNAR | .5767** | .7618** | .7879** | .8436** | .8198** | .6531** | .8649** | .9128** | .8216** | .9191** | 1.0000 | .9590** |
| ESSAY | .7441** | .7872** | .7877** | .7713** | .7503** | .8409** | .8791** | .8350** | .9330** | .9700** | .9590** | 1.0000 |

\* signif. ≤ .01.
\*\* signif. ≤ .001.

*Table F.7. Correlations of major variables, Sample C*

| | SATV | SATM | SATR | SATVOC | TSWE | ECT | COURSE | DISC | MECH | WRSKILL | NAR1 |
|---|---|---|---|---|---|---|---|---|---|---|---|
| SATV | 1.0000 | .5427** | .9360** | .9352** | .6853** | .7008** | .3684** | .2955** | .3417** | .3602** | .5966** |
| SATM | .5427** | 1.0000 | .4984** | .5161** | .4790** | .4933** | .1375 | .1163 | .1306 | .1395 | .3414** |
| SATR | .9360** | .4984** | 1.0000 | .7575** | .6424** | .6528** | .3375** | .2716** | .3094** | .3284** | .5350** |
| SATVOC | .9352** | .5161** | .7575** | 1.0000 | .6504** | .6571** | .3564** | .2811** | .3151** | .3370** | .5822** |
| TSWE | .6853** | .4790** | .6424** | .6504** | 1.0000 | .8347** | .4238** | .3245** | .4776** | .4538** | .6978** |
| ECT | .7008** | .4933** | .6528** | .6571** | .8347** | 1.0000 | .4051** | .3234** | .4986** | .4652** | .6520** |
| COURSE | .3684** | .1375 | .3375** | .3564** | .4238** | .4051** | 1.0000 | .8673** | .6668** | .8656** | .4727** |
| DISC | .2955** | .1163 | .2716** | .2811** | .3245** | .3234** | .8673** | 1.0000 | .5669** | .8830** | .3498** |
| MECH | .3417** | .1306 | .3094** | .3151** | .4776** | .4986** | .6668** | .5669** | 1.0000 | .8872** | .4641** |
| WRSKILL | .3602** | .1395 | .3284** | .3370** | .4538** | .4652** | .8656** | .8830** | .8872** | 1.0000 | .4603** |
| NAR1 | .5966** | .3414** | .5350** | .5822** | .6978** | .6520** | .4727** | .3498** | .4641** | .4603** | 1.0000 |
| NAR2 | .3703** | .1355 | .3429** | .3321** | .4792** | .4199** | .5022** | .4491** | .4262** | .4944** | .5648** |
| EXP1 | .4605** | .2518* | .4274** | .4224** | .5587** | .4993** | .4552** | .3556** | .3874** | .4199** | .6059** |
| EXP2 | .4086** | .3113** | .3872** | .3849** | .5309** | .4772** | .4886** | .3983** | .4247** | .4650** | .5632** |
| PER1 | .3042** | .2279* | .2794** | .2839** | .4489** | .4019** | .5166** | .3955** | .5461** | .5326** | .4673** |
| PER2 | .3545** | .2800** | .3341** | .3211** | .4891** | .4594** | .5339** | .4563** | .5460** | .5666** | .5199** |
| NARTOTAL | .5437** | .2670** | .4938** | .5136** | .6625** | .6029** | .5514** | .4528** | .5027** | .5400** | .8791** |
| EXPTOTAL | .4802** | .3100** | .4500** | .4459** | .6016** | .5391** | .5204** | .4155** | .4476** | .4877** | .6456** |
| PERTOTAL | .3619** | .2787** | .3368** | .3325** | .5158** | .4732** | .5783** | .4680** | .6016** | .6048** | .5427** |
| NOTPER | .5543** | .3110** | .5107** | .5196** | .6841** | .6182** | .5796** | .4698** | .5144** | .5562** | .8279** |
| NOTEXP | .5133** | .3102** | .4709** | .4795** | .6686** | .6106** | .6422** | .5234** | .6284** | .6512** | .8055** |
| NOTNAR | .4710** | .3306** | .4400** | .4353** | .6269** | .5682** | .6200** | .4987** | .5946** | .6181** | .6663** |
| ESSAY | .5354** | .3309** | .4946** | .4991** | .6886** | .6251** | .6403** | .5187** | .6039** | .6345** | .8005** |

Table F.7. continued

| | NAR2 | EXP1 | EXP2 | PER1 | PER2 | NARTOTAL | EXPTOTAL | PERTOTAL | NOTPER | NOTEXP | NOTNAR | ESSAY |
|---|---|---|---|---|---|---|---|---|---|---|---|---|
| SATV | .3703** | .4605** | .4086** | .3042** | .3545** | .5437** | .4802** | .3619** | .5543** | .5133** | .4710** | .5354** |
| SATM | .1355 | .2518* | .3113** | .2279** | .2800** | .2570** | .3100** | .2787** | .3110** | .3102** | .3306** | .3309** |
| SATR | .3429** | .4274** | .3872** | .2794** | .3341** | .4438** | .4500** | .3368** | .5107** | .4709** | .4400** | .4946** |
| SATVCO | .3321** | .4224** | .3849** | .2839** | .3211** | .5.36** | .4459** | .3325** | .5196** | .4795** | .4353** | .4991** |
| TSWE | .4792** | .5587** | .5309** | .4489** | .4891** | .6825** | .6016** | .5158** | .6841** | .6686** | .6269** | .6886** |
| ECT | .4199** | .4993** | .4772** | .4019** | .4594** | .6029** | .5391** | .4732** | .6182** | .6106** | .5682** | .6251** |
| COURSE | .5022** | .4552** | .4886** | .5166** | .5339** | .5514** | .5204** | .5783** | .5796** | .6422** | .6200** | .6403** |
| DISC | .4491** | .3556** | .3983** | .3955** | .4563** | .4828** | .4155** | .4680** | .4698** | .5234** | .4987** | .5187** |
| MECH | .4262** | .3874** | .4247** | .5461** | .5460** | .5027** | .4476** | .6016** | .5144** | .6284** | .5946** | .6039** |
| WRSKILL | .4944** | .4199** | .4650** | .5326** | .5666** | .5400** | .4877** | .6048** | .5562** | .6512** | .6181** | .6345** |
| NAR1 | .5648** | .6059** | .5632** | .4673** | .5199** | .8791** | .6456** | .5427** | .8279** | .8055** | .6663** | .8005** |
| NAR2 | 1.0000 | .6001** | .5134** | .3416** | .4411** | .8899** | .6155** | .4291** | .8181** | .7461** | .5833** | .7479** |
| EXP1 | .6001** | 1.0000 | .6421** | .4273** | .4671** | .6826** | .9103** | .4918** | .8562** | .6655** | .7786** | .7999** |
| EXP2 | .5134** | .6421** | 1.0000 | .5378** | .4667** | .6079** | .9018** | .5548** | .8106** | .6604** | .8111** | .7932** |
| PER1 | .3416** | .4273** | .5378** | 1.0000 | .6474** | .4556** | .5312** | .9147** | .5318** | .7823** | .8238** | .7422** |
| PER2 | .4411** | .4671** | .4667** | .6474** | 1.0000 | .5422** | .5153** | .9002** | .5718** | .8225** | .8068** | .7645** |
| NARTOTAL | .8899** | .6816** | .6079** | .4556** | .5422** | 1.0000 | .7124** | .5479** | .9302** | .8762** | .7053** | .8745** |
| EXPTOTAL | .6155** | .9103** | .9018** | .5312** | .5153** | .7124** | 1.0000 | .5767** | .9202** | .7316** | .8768** | .8791** |
| PERTOTAL | .4291** | .4918** | .5548** | .9147** | .9002** | .5479** | .5767** | 1.0000 | .6071** | .8832** | .8985** | .8295** |
| NOTPER | .8181** | .8562** | .8106** | .5318** | .5718** | .9302** | .9202** | .6071** | 1.0000 | .8713** | .8518** | .9474** |
| NOTEXP | .7461** | .6655** | .6604** | .7823** | .8225** | .8762** | .7316** | .8832** | .8713** | 1.0000 | .9130** | .9681** |
| NOTNAR | .5833** | .7786** | .8111** | .8238** | .8068** | .7053** | .8768** | .8985** | .8518** | .9130** | 1.0000 | .9606** |
| ESSAY | .7479** | .7999** | .7932** | .7422** | .7645** | .8745** | .8791** | .8295** | .9474** | .9681** | .9606** | 1.0000 |

\* signif. ≤ .01.
\*\* signif. ≤ .001.

*Table F.8. Correlations of major variables, Sample D*

| | SATV | SATM | SATR | SATVOC | TSWE | ECT | COURSE | DISC | MECH | WRSKILL | NAR1 |
|---|---|---|---|---|---|---|---|---|---|---|---|
| SATV | 1.0000 | .5876** | .9345** | .9305** | .6883** | .7431** | .4161** | .3410** | .3826** | .4197** | .6178** |
| SATM | .5876** | 1.0000 | .5385** | .5523** | .5614** | .5765** | .1201 | .1203 | .1446 | .1538 | .3953** |
| SATR | .9345** | .5385** | 1.0000 | .7458** | .6412** | .7034** | .3728** | .2989** | .3437** | .3729** | .5616** |
| SATVOC | .9305** | .5523** | .7458** | 1.0000 | .6534** | .6830** | .4120** | .3449** | .3612** | .4089** | .5930** |
| TSWE | .6883** | .5614** | .6412** | .6534** | 1.0000 | .8673** | .4488** | .3140* | .4971** | .4739** | .7320** |
| ECT | .7431** | .5765** | .7034** | .6830** | .8673** | 1.0000 | .4441** | .3441** | .5456** | .5199** | .6817** |
| COURSE | .4161** | .1201 | .3728** | .4120** | .4488** | .4441** | 1.0000 | .8319** | .6540** | .8551** | .4925** |
| DISC | .3410** | .1203 | .2989* | .3449** | .3140* | .3441** | .8319** | 1.0000 | .4928** | .8508** | .3264** |
| MECH | .3826** | .1446 | .3437** | .3612** | .4971** | .5456** | .6540** | .4928** | 1.0000 | .8766** | .4235** |
| WRSKILL | .4197** | .1538 | .3729** | .4089** | .4739** | .5199** | .8551** | .8508** | .8766** | 1.0000 | .4363** |
| NAR1 | .6178** | .3953** | .5616** | .5930** | .7320** | .6817** | .4925** | .3264** | .4235** | .4363** | 1.0000 |
| NAR2 | .4223** | .2095 | .3895** | .3838** | .5311** | .4727** | .5470** | .4221** | .4121** | .4823** | .5843** |
| EXP1 | .4980** | .3002* | .4634** | .4555** | .5707** | .5073** | .5333** | .3593** | .4196** | .4522** | .6356** |
| EXP2 | .4857** | .3669** | .4513** | .4624** | .5512** | .5184** | .5025** | .3489** | .4291** | .4521** | .5599** |
| PER1 | .3238** | .2184 | .3023* | .2927 | .4488** | .4671** | .4890** | .2968** | .5116** | .4732** | .4397** |
| PER2 | .3377** | .2093 | .3190** | .3029* | .4867** | .4677** | .4676** | .2815* | .5309** | .4764** | .5227** |
| NARTOTAL | .5828** | .3383** | .5330** | .5470** | .7080** | .6468** | .5844** | .4212** | .4693** | .5164** | .8867** |
| EXPTOTAL | .5356** | .3597** | .4980** | .4989** | .6111** | .5573** | .5647** | .3857** | .4611** | .4918** | .6537** |
| PERTOTAL | .3586** | .2327 | .3367** | .3230** | .5065** | .5076** | .5205** | .3147* | .5654** | .5155** | .5191** |
| NOTPER | .6049** | .3767** | .5575** | .5658** | .7141** | .6519** | .6211** | .4364** | .5027** | .5450** | .8357** |
| NOTEXP | .5406** | .3275** | .4993** | .4998** | .6963** | .6611** | .6318** | .4217** | .5895** | .5893** | .8077** |
| NOTNAR | .4998** | .3311** | .4666** | .4584** | .6250** | .5957** | .6070** | .3917** | .5745** | .5637** | .6558** |
| ESSAY | .5726** | .3602** | .5302** | .5309** | .7077** | .6634** | .6461** | .4345** | .5780** | .5894** | .8002** |
| WORDS | .2323 | .2332 | .2263 | .2117 | .3547** | .2593* | .4578** | .3088* | .2797 | .3397** | .4915** |
| R12ABC | -.5020** | -.3552** | -.4323** | -.5064** | -.6883** | -.6342** | -.5480** | -.4019** | -.4815** | -.5131** | -.6908** |
| R12DEF | -.2248 | -.1425 | -.1643 | -.2344 | -.4113** | -.3974** | -.3285** | -.1189 | -.4277** | -.3241** | -.4265** |
| R12TOT | -.3993** | -.2723* | -.3258** | -.4076** | -.6112** | -.5746** | -.4873** | -.2820* | -.5141** | -.4665** | -.6219** |

*Table F.8. continued*

| | NAR2 | EXP1 | EXP2 | PER1 | PER2 | NARTOTAL | EXPTOTAL | PERTOTAL | NOTPER | NOTEXP | NOTNAR |
|---|---|---|---|---|---|---|---|---|---|---|---|
| SATV | .4223** | .4980** | .4857** | .3238** | .3?77** | .5828** | .5356** | .3586** | .6049** | .5406** | .4998** |
| SATM | .2095 | .3002** | .3669** | .2184 | .2?93 | .3383** | .3597** | .2327 | .3767** | .3275** | .3311** |
| SATR | .3895** | .4634** | .4513** | .3023* | .3?90** | .5330** | .4980** | .3367** | .5575** | .4993** | .4666** |
| SATVOC | .3838** | .4555** | .4624** | .2927* | .3?29* | .5470** | .4989** | .3230** | .5658** | .4998** | .4594** |
| TSWE | .5311** | .5707** | .5512** | .4488** | .4?67** | .7080** | .6111** | .5065** | .7141** | .6963** | .6250** |
| ECT | .4727** | .5073** | .5184** | .4671** | .4?77** | .6468** | .5573** | .5076** | .6519** | .6611** | .5957** |
| COURSE | .5470** | .5333** | .5025** | .4890** | .4?76** | .5844** | .5647** | .5205** | .6211** | .6318** | .6070** |
| DISC | .4221** | .3593** | .3489** | .2968* | .2?15* | .4212** | .3857** | .3147* | .4364** | .4217** | .3917** |
| MECH | .4121** | .4196** | .4291** | .5116** | .5?09*** | .4693** | .4611** | .5654** | .5027** | .5895** | .5745** |
| WRSKILL | .4823** | .4522** | .4521** | .4732** | .4?54** | .5164** | .4918** | .5155** | .5450** | .5893** | .5637** |
| NAR1 | .5843** | .6356** | .5599** | .4397** | .5227** | .8867** | .6537** | .5191** | .8357** | .8077** | .6558** |
| NAR2 | 1.0000 | .6016** | .5248** | .3796** | .4?59** | .8933** | .6162** | .4310** | .8196** | .7624** | .5854** |
| EXP1 | .6016** | 1.0000 | .6882** | .5074** | .4?55** | .6948** | .9326** | .5402** | .8756** | .7073** | .8230** |
| EXP2 | .5248** | .6882** | 1.0000 | .5884** | .4?01** | .6090** | .9036** | .5600** | .8127** | .6682** | .8180** |
| PER1 | .3796** | .5074** | .5884** | 1.0000 | .6?3** | .4598** | .5922** | .9329** | .5663** | .7889** | .8541** |
| PER2 | .4169** | .4855** | .4301** | .6933** | 1.0000 | .5270** | .5005** | .9063** | .5555** | .8134** | .7881** |
| NARTOTAL | .8933** | .6943** | .6090** | .4598** | .5?0** | 1.0000 | .7131** | .5330** | .9298** | .8817** | .6967** |
| EXPTOTAL | .6162** | .9326** | .9036** | .5922** | .5?05** | .7131** | 1.0000 | .5974** | .9211** | .7499** | .8927** |
| PERTOTAL | .4310** | .5402** | .5600** | .9329** | .9?63** | .5330** | .5974** | 1.0000 | .6097** | .8691** | .8947** |
| NOTPER | .8196** | .8756** | .8127** | .5663** | .5?5** | .9298** | .9211** | .6097** | 1.0000 | .8834** | .8557** |
| NOTEXP | .7624** | .7073** | .6682** | .7889** | .8?4** | .8817** | .7499** | .8691** | .8834** | 1.0000 | .9061** |
| NOTNAR | .5854** | .8230** | .8180** | .8541** | .7?1** | .6967** | .8927** | .8947** | .8557** | .9061** | 1.0000 |
| ESSAY | .7550** | .8370** | .7992** | .7640** | .7?4** | .8733** | .8916** | .8209** | .9531** | .9682** | .9579** |
| WORDS | .5138** | .5391** | .5713** | .5243** | .5?9** | .5649** | .6024** | .5668** | .6300** | .6463** | .6541** |
| R12ABC | -.6137** | -.6769** | -.5978** | -.5841** | -.5?25** | -.7322** | -.6969** | -.6187** | -.7726** | -.7729** | -.7358** |
| R12DEF | -.4648** | -.5217** | -.5193** | -.4947** | -.4?13** | -.5010** | -.5663** | -.5159** | -.5756** | -.5805** | -.6053** |
| R12TOT | -.6056** | -.6735** | -.6310** | -.6087** | -.565?** | -.6894** | -.7115** | -.6397** | -.7565** | -.7597** | -.7558** |

*Continued on next page*

## Table F.8. continued

|  | ESSAY | WORDS | R12ABC | R12DEF | R12TOT |
|---|---|---|---|---|---|
| SATV | .5726** | .2323 | −.5020** | −.2248 | −.3993** |
| SATM | .3602** | .2332 | −.3552** | −.1425 | −.2723* |
| SATR | .5302** | .2263 | −.4323** | −.1643 | −.3258** |
| SATVOC | .5309** | .2117 | −.5064** | −.2344 | −.4076** |
| TSWE | .7077** | .3547** | −.6883** | −.4113** | −.6112** |
| ECT | .6634** | .2593* | −.6342** | −.3974** | −.5746** |
| COURSE | .6461** | .4578** | −.5480** | −.3285** | −.4873** |
| DISC | .4345** | .3088* | −.4019** | −.1189 | −.2820* |
| MECH | .5780** | .2797* | −.4815** | −.4277** | −.5141** |
| WRSKILL | .5894** | .3397** | −.5131** | −.3241** | −.4665** |
| NAR1 | .8002** | .4915** | −.6908** | −.4265** | −.6219** |
| NAR2 | .7550** | .5138** | −.6137** | −.4648** | −.6056** |
| EXP1 | .8370** | .5391** | −.6769** | −.5217** | −.6753** |
| EXP2 | .7992** | .5713** | −.5978** | −.5193** | −.6310** |
| PER1 | .7640** | .5243** | −.5841** | −.4947** | −.6087** |
| PER2 | .7461** | .5191** | −.5525** | −.4518** | −.5658** |
| NARTOTAL | .8733** | .5649** | −.7322** | −.5010** | −.6894** |
| EXPTOTAL | .8916** | .6024** | −.6969** | −.5663** | −.7115** |
| PERTOTAL | .8209** | .5668** | −.6187** | −.5159** | −.6397** |
| NOTPER | .9531** | .6300** | −.7726** | −.5756** | −.7565** |
| NOTEXP | .9682** | .6463** | −.7729** | −.5805** | −.7597** |
| NOTNAR | .9579** | .6541** | −.7358** | −.6053** | −.7558** |
| ESSAY | 1.0000 | .6703** | −.7927** | −.6116** | −.7891** |
| WORDS | .6703** | 1.0000 | −.4842** | −.3073** | −.4411** |
| R12ABC | −.7927** | −.4842** | 1.0000 | .5444** | .8552** |
| R12DEF | −.6116** | −.3073* | .5444** | 1.0000 | .9004** |
| R12TOT | −.7891** | −.4411** | .8552** | .9004** | 1.0000 |

&ast; signif. ≤ .01.
&ast;&ast; signif. ≤ .001.

## Table F.9. Multiple correlations between alternative predictor sets and writing performance (WP) criterion for Sample A (267 cases)

| Predictor(s) | Criteria[a] | | | | | | | Average R |
| | WP | WP1 | WP2 | WP3 | WP4 | WP5 | WP6 | |
|---|---|---|---|---|---|---|---|---|
| TSWE (1) | .63 | .59 | .62 | .62 | .63 | .62 | .64 | .62 |
| SAT-V (2) | .55 | .52 | .55 | .53 | .54 | .55 | .55 | .54 |
| ECT (3) | | | | | | | | |
| Essay[b]—one reading (4) | | .51 | .53 | .57 | .57 | .55 | .52 | .54 |
| Essay[b]—two readings (5) | | .58 | .60 | .64 | .64 | .61 | .58 | .61 |
| Essay[b]—three readings (6) | | .62 | .64 | .67 | .67 | .63 | .60 | .64 |
| *Combinations* | | | | | | | | |
| 1,2 | | .61 | .64 | .63 | .65 | .64 | .65 | .64 |
| 1,4 | | .65 | .70 | .70 | .73 | .70 | .71 | .70 |
| 1,5 | | .67 | .72 | .73 | .75 | .72 | .73 | .72 |
| 1,6 | | .68 | .74 | .74 | .77 | .72 | .74 | .73 |
| 2,4 | | .61 | .66 | .66 | .68 | .67 | .67 | .66 |
| 2,5 | | .65 | .70 | .69 | .71 | .70 | .69 | .69 |
| 2,6 | | .66 | .72 | .71 | .73 | .71 | .71 | .71 |
| 1,2,4 | | .66 | .71 | .71 | .73 | .71 | .72 | .71 |
| 1,2,5 | | .68 | .73 | .73 | .76 | .73 | .74 | .73 |
| 1,2,6 | | .69 | .75 | .74 | .77 | .74 | .75 | .74 |

a.  WP  = sum of holistic scores for six essays
   WP1 = sum of holistic scores for five essays, excluding N1 (Family Traditions)
   WP2 = sum of holistic scores for five essays, excluding N2 (Significant Event)
   WP3 = sum of holistic scores for five essays, excluding E1 (Status Symbols)
   WP4 = sum of holistic scores for five essays, excluding E2 (Cornerstone)
   WP5 = sum of holistic scores for five essays, excluding P1 (Drinking and Driving)
   WP6 = sum of holistic scores for five essays, excluding P2 (Book Censorship)
b.  Specific essay used is always the essay not included in the criterion.

## Table F.10. Multiple correlations between alternative predictor sets and writing performance (WP) criterion for Sample B (210 cases)

| Predictor(s) | Criteria[a] | | | | | | | Average R |
| --- | --- | --- | --- | --- | --- | --- | --- | --- |
| | WP | WP1 | WP2 | WP3 | WP4 | WP5 | WP6 | |
| TSWE (1) | .63 | .60 | .63 | .61 | .63 | .62 | .64 | .62 |
| SAT-V (2) | .54 | .51 | .54 | .53 | .53 | .53 | .55 | .53 |
| ECT (3) | .61 | .58 | .62 | .61 | .61 | .58 | .61 | .60 |
| Essay[b]—one reading (4) | | .52 | .52 | .59 | .59 | .56 | .53 | .55 |
| Essay[b]—two readings (5) | | .59 | .59 | .66 | .66 | .61 | .59 | .62 |
| Essay[b]—three readings (6) | | .62 | .62 | .69 | .69 | .63 | .61 | .64 |
| *Combinations* | | | | | | | | |
| 1,2 | | .62 | .65 | .63 | .64 | .63 | .66 | .64 |
| 1,3 | | .62 | .66 | .65 | .65 | .63 | .66 | .65 |
| 2,3 | | .60 | .64 | .63 | .63 | .61 | .64 | .63 |
| 1,4 | | .66 | .71 | .71 | .72 | .70 | .72 | .70 |
| 1,5 | | .68 | .73 | .74 | .75 | .72 | .74 | .73 |
| 1,6 | | .69 | .74 | .75 | .77 | .72 | .75 | .74 |
| 2,4 | | .62 | .66 | .67 | .68 | .66 | .67 | .66 |
| 2,5 | | .65 | .69 | .71 | .72 | .69 | .70 | .69 |
| 2,6 | | .67 | .71 | .73 | .74 | .70 | .71 | .71 |
| 3,4 | | .64 | .71 | .72 | .71 | .67 | .70 | .69 |
| 3,5 | | .67 | .73 | .75 | .75 | .69 | .72 | .72 |
| 3,6 | | .68 | .75 | .76 | .76 | .70 | .73 | .73 |
| 1,2,4 | | .67 | .72 | .72 | .73 | .71 | .73 | .71 |
| 1,3,4 | | .67 | .73 | .73 | .73 | .70 | .73 | .72 |
| 2,3,4 | | .66 | .72 | .72 | .72 | .69 | .71 | .70 |
| 1,2,5 | | .69 | .74 | .74 | .76 | .72 | .75 | .73 |
| 1,3,5 | | .69 | .75 | .75 | .76 | .72 | .75 | .74 |
| 2,3,5 | | .68 | .74 | .75 | .75 | .71 | .73 | .73 |
| 1,2,6 | | .70 | .75 | .75 | .77 | .73 | .76 | .74 |
| 1,3,6 | | .70 | .76 | .77 | .77 | .73 | .76 | .75 |
| 2,3,6 | | .69 | .75 | .77 | .77 | .72 | .74 | .74 |

a. See note a in Table F.9.
b. See note b in Table F.9.

*Table F.11. Multiple correlations between alternative predictor sets and writing performance (WP) criterion for Sample C (141 cases)*

| Predictor(s) | Criteria[a] | | | | | | | Average R |
| --- | --- | --- | --- | --- | --- | --- | --- | --- |
| | WP | WP1 | WP2 | WP3 | WP4 | WP5 | WP6 | |
| TSWE (1) | .69 | .64 | .69 | .68 | .69 | .69 | .69 | .68 |
| SAT-V (2) | .54 | .49 | .54 | .52 | .53 | .55 | .54 | .53 |
| ECT (3) | .62 | .58 | .63 | .62 | .62 | .63 | .62 | .62 |
| Essay[b]—one reading (4) | | .58 | .52 | .60 | .60 | .53 | .54 | .56 |
| Essay[b]—two readings (5) | | .66 | .59 | .67 | .67 | .59 | .61 | .63 |
| Essay[b]—three readings (6) | | .70 | .62 | .70 | .70 | .61 | .65 | .66 |
| *Combinations* | | | | | | | | |
| 1,2 | | .65 | .69 | .68 | .69 | .70 | .70 | .69 |
| 1,3 | | .65 | .69 | .69 | .69 | .70 | .69 | .69 |
| 2,3 | | .59 | .64 | .63 | .64 | .65 | .64 | .63 |
| 1,4 | | .69 | .74 | .75 | .76 | .75 | .74 | .74 |
| 1,5 | | .72 | .75 | .77 | .78 | .76 | .77 | .76 |
| 1,6 | | .73 | .76 | .78 | .79 | .77 | .78 | .77 |
| 2,4 | | .62 | .65 | .68 | .69 | .68 | .67 | .67 |
| 2,5 | | .68 | .68 | .72 | .73 | .71 | .71 | .71 |
| 2,6 | | .70 | .70 | .74 | .75 | .72 | .73 | .72 |
| 3,4 | | .66 | .70 | .72 | .73 | .71 | .70 | .70 |
| 3,5 | | .70 | .73 | .75 | .76 | .73 | .73 | .73 |
| 3,6 | | .72 | .74 | .77 | .77 | .74 | .74 | .75 |
| 1,2,4 | | .69 | .74 | .75 | .76 | .76 | .75 | .74 |
| 1,3,4 | | .69 | .74 | .75 | .76 | .75 | .75 | .74 |
| 2,3,4 | | .66 | .71 | .72 | .73 | .73 | .71 | .71 |
| 1,2,5 | | .72 | .76 | .77 | .78 | .77 | .77 | .76 |
| 1,3,5 | | .72 | .76 | .77 | .78 | .77 | .77 | .76 |
| 2,3,5 | | .70 | .73 | .75 | .76 | .75 | .74 | .74 |
| 1,2,6 | | .73 | .77 | .78 | .79 | .78 | .78 | .77 |
| 1,3,6 | | .73 | .77 | .79 | .79 | .77 | .78 | .77 |
| 2,3,6 | | .72 | .74 | .77 | .78 | .75 | .76 | .75 |

a. See note a in Table F.9.
b. See note b in Table F.9.

## Table F.12. Multiple correlations between alternative predictor sets and writing performance (WP) criterion for Sample D (94 cases)

| Predictor(s) | Criteria[a] | | | | | | | Average R |
|---|---|---|---|---|---|---|---|---|
| | WP | WP1 | WP2 | WP3 | WP4 | WP5 | WP6 | |
| TSWE (1) | .71 | .66 | .70 | .71 | .71 | .72 | .71 | .70 |
| SAT-V (2) | .57 | .52 | .57 | .56 | .56 | .59 | .59 | .57 |
| ECT (3) | .66 | .62 | .66 | .67 | .66 | .66 | .66 | .66 |
| Essay[b]—one reading (4) | | .59 | .54 | .65 | .59 | .56 | .50 | .57 |
| Essay[b]—two readings (5) | | .66 | .60 | .72 | .68 | .62 | .59 | .65 |
| Essay[b]—three readings (6) | | .69 | .63 | .75 | .71 | .64 | .64 | .68 |
| *Combinations* | | | | | | | | |
| 1,2 | | .66 | .71 | .71 | .71 | .73 | .72 | .71 |
| 1,3 | | .66 | .71 | .71 | .71 | .73 | .72 | .71 |
| 2,3 | | .62 | .67 | .68 | .67 | .68 | .68 | .67 |
| 1,4 | | .70 | .74 | .79 | .77 | .78 | .75 | .76 |
| 1,5 | | .72 | .75 | .81 | .79 | .80 | .77 | .77 |
| 1,6 | | .73 | .76 | .82 | .80 | .80 | .79 | .78 |
| 2,4 | | .64 | .66 | .72 | .69 | .72 | .69 | .69 |
| 2,5 | | .68 | .70 | .76 | .73 | .75 | .73 | .73 |
| 2,6 | | .70 | .71 | .78 | .75 | .76 | .75 | .74 |
| 3,4 | | .68 | .72 | .78 | .74 | .74 | .72 | .73 |
| 3,5 | | .71 | .74 | .81 | .77 | .76 | .75 | .76 |
| 3,6 | | .72 | .75 | .82 | .79 | .76 | .76 | .77 |
| 1,2,4 | | .70 | .68 | .79 | .77 | .79 | .77 | .75 |
| 1,3,4 | | .70 | .75 | .79 | .77 | .78 | .76 | .76 |
| 2,3,4 | | .68 | .73 | .78 | .75 | .76 | .73 | .74 |
| 1,2,5 | | .72 | .76 | .81 | .79 | .81 | .78 | .78 |
| 1,3,5 | | .72 | .76 | .82 | .80 | .80 | .78 | .78 |
| 2,3,5 | | .71 | .75 | .81 | .78 | .77 | .76 | .76 |
| 1,2,6 | | .73 | .77 | .82 | .81 | .81 | .80 | .79 |
| 1,3,6 | | .73 | .77 | .83 | .81 | .80 | .79 | .79 |
| 2,3,6 | | .72 | .75 | .82 | .79 | .78 | .77 | .77 |

a. See note a in Table F.9.
b. See note b in Table F.9.

## Table F.13. Multiple correlations between alternative predictor sets and instructors' judgments of writing skill for Sample A (267 cases)

| Predictor(s) | Essay used as predictor[a] | | | | | | | Average |
| | None | N1 | N2 | E1 | E2 | P1 | P2 | R |
| --- | --- | --- | --- | --- | --- | --- | --- | --- |
| TSWE (1) | .48 | | | | | | | |
| SAT-V (2) | .46 | | | | | | | |
| ECT (3) | — | | | | | | | |
| Essay[b]—one reading (4) | | .39 | .41 | .35 | .41 | .49 | .47 | .42 |
| Essay[b]—two readings (5) | | .43 | .47 | .39 | .46 | .54 | .52 | .47 |
| Essay[b]—three readings (6) | | .46 | .49 | .41 | .48 | .57 | .55 | .49 |
| *Combinations* | | | | | | | | |
| 1,2 | .51 | | | | | | | |
| 1,4 | | .51 | .54 | .50 | .54 | .58 | .58 | .54 |
| 1,5 | | .52 | .56 | .51 | .55 | .60 | .60 | .56 |
| 1,6 | | .53 | .57 | .51 | .56 | .61 | .61 | .57 |
| 2,4 | | .51 | .54 | .49 | .53 | .58 | .57 | .54 |
| 2,5 | | .52 | .56 | .50 | .55 | .61 | .60 | .56 |
| 2,6 | | .53 | .57 | .51 | .56 | .62 | .62 | .57 |
| 1,2,4 | | .53 | .56 | .53 | .55 | .60 | .59 | .56 |
| 1,2,5 | | .54 | .58 | .53 | .57 | .62 | .62 | .58 |
| 1,2,6 | | .54 | .58 | .53 | .58 | .63 | .63 | .58 |

a. N1 = first narrative essay (Family Traditions)
   N2 = second narrative essay (Significant Event)
   E1 = first expository essay (Status Symbols)
   E2 = second expository essay (Cornerstone)
   P1 = first persuasive essay (Drinking and Driving)
   P2 = second persuasive essay (Book Censorship)
b. Specific essay used is always the essay not included in the criterion.

## Table F.14. Multiple correlations between alternative predictor sets and instructors' judgments of writing skill for Sample B (210 cases)

| Predictor(s) | Essay used as predictor[a] | | | | | | | Average R |
| | None | N1 | N2 | E1 | E2 | P1 | P2 | |
| --- | --- | --- | --- | --- | --- | --- | --- | --- |
| TSWE (1) | .49 | | | | | | | |
| SAT-V (2) | .47 | | | | | | | |
| ECT (3) | .50 | | | | | | | |
| Essay[b]—one reading (4) | | .38 | .40 | .38 | .45 | .50 | .45 | .36 |
| Essay[b]—two readings (5) | | .43 | .46 | .42 | .50 | .55 | .50 | .48 |
| Essay[b]—three readings (6) | | .45 | .48 | .44 | .53 | .58 | .52 | .50 |
| *Combinations* | | | | | | | | |
| 1,2 | .52 | | | | | | | |
| 1,3 | .52 | | | | | | | |
| 2,3 | .53 | | | | | | | |
| 1,4 | | .52 | .55 | .52 | .56 | .59 | .57 | .55 |
| 1,5 | | .53 | .56 | .53 | .58 | .61 | .59 | .57 |
| 1,6 | | .53 | .57 | .53 | .59 | .62 | .61 | .58 |
| 2,4 | | .52 | .55 | .52 | .55 | .59 | .57 | .55 |
| 2,5 | | .53 | .57 | .53 | .58 | .62 | .59 | .57 |
| 2,6 | | .54 | .58 | .54 | .59 | .63 | .61 | .58 |
| 3,4 | | .53 | .57 | .54 | .57 | .59 | .58 | .56 |
| 3,5 | | .54 | .58 | .55 | .59 | .61 | .60 | .58 |
| 3,6 | | .55 | .59 | .56 | .60 | .62 | .61 | .59 |
| 1,2,4 | | .54 | .57 | .54 | .58 | .61 | .59 | .57 |
| 1,3,4 | | .54 | .57 | .55 | .58 | .60 | .59 | .57 |
| 2,3,4 | | .55 | .59 | .56 | .59 | .61 | .60 | .58 |
| 1,2,5 | | .55 | .59 | .55 | .59 | .63 | .61 | .59 |
| 1,3,5 | | .55 | .59 | .56 | .60 | .62 | .61 | .59 |
| 2,3,5 | | .56 | .60 | .57 | .60 | .63 | .62 | .60 |
| 1,2,6 | | .55 | .59 | .55 | .60 | .64 | .62 | .59 |
| 1,3,6 | | .55 | .60 | .56 | .61 | .63 | .62 | .60 |
| 2,3,6 | | .56 | .61 | .57 | .61 | .64 | .63 | .60 |

a. See note a in Table F.13.
b. See note b in Table F.13.

*Table F.15. Multiple correlations between alternative predictor sets and instructors' judgments of writing skill for Sample C (141 cases)*

| Predictor(s) | Essay used as predictor[a] | | | | | | | Average R |
|---|---|---|---|---|---|---|---|---|
| | None | N1 | N2 | E1 | E2 | P1 | P2 | |
| TSWE (1) | .45 | | | | | | | |
| SAT-V (2) | .36 | | | | | | | |
| ECT (3) | .47 | | | | | | | |
| Essay[b]—one reading (4) | | .39 | .42 | .35 | .40 | .46 | .47 | .42 |
| Essay[b]—two readings (5) | | .44 | .47 | .40 | .44 | .51 | .53 | .47 |
| Essay[b]—three readings (6) | | .46 | .49 | .42 | .47 | .53 | .57 | .49 |
| *Combinations* | | | | | | | | |
| 1,2 | .46 | | | | | | | |
| 1,3 | .48 | | | | | | | |
| 2,3 | .47 | | | | | | | |
| 1,4 | | .48 | .52 | .49 | .50 | .55 | .55 | .52 |
| 1,5 | | .49 | .54 | .49 | .52 | .57 | .58 | .53 |
| 1,6 | | .50 | .55 | .50 | .53 | .58 | .60 | .54 |
| 2,4 | | .43 | .48 | .43 | .46 | .53 | .52 | .48 |
| 2,5 | | .46 | .51 | .45 | .49 | .56 | .57 | .51 |
| 2,6 | | .47 | .53 | .46 | .50 | .57 | .59 | .52 |
| 3,4 | | .49 | .54 | .50 | .52 | .57 | .56 | .53 |
| 3,5 | | .50 | .56 | .51 | .53 | .59 | .59 | .55 |
| 3,6 | | .51 | .57 | .51 | .54 | .60 | .61 | .56 |
| 1,2,4 | | .48 | .53 | .49 | .47 | .56 | .55 | .51 |
| 1,3,4 | | .50 | .54 | .51 | .52 | .57 | .57 | .54 |
| 2,3,4 | | .49 | .54 | .50 | .52 | .57 | .56 | .53 |
| 1,2,5 | | .49 | .54 | .50 | .52 | .58 | .59 | .54 |
| 1,3,5 | | .51 | .56 | .51 | .54 | .59 | .60 | .55 |
| 2,3,5 | | .50 | .56 | .51 | .53 | .59 | .60 | .55 |
| 1,2,6 | | .50 | .55 | .50 | .53 | .59 | .60 | .55 |
| 1,3,6 | | .51 | .57 | .52 | .54 | .60 | .61 | .56 |
| 2,3,6 | | .51 | .57 | .51 | .54 | .60 | .61 | .56 |

a. See note a in Table F.13.
b. See note b in Table F.13.

*Table F.16. Multiple correlations between alternative predictor sets and instructors' judgments of writing skill for Sample D (94 cases)*

| Predictor(s) | Essay used as predictor[a] | | | | | | | Average R |
| | None | N1 | N2 | E1 | E2 | P1 | P2 | |
| --- | --- | --- | --- | --- | --- | --- | --- | --- |
| TSWE (1) | .47 | | | | | | | |
| SAT-V (2) | .42 | | | | | | | |
| ECT (3) | .52 | | | | | | | |
| Essay[b]—one reading (4) | | .37 | .41 | .39 | .38 | .41 | .37 | .39 |
| Essay[b]—two readings (5) | | .42 | .46 | .44 | .43 | .46 | .44 | .44 |
| Essay[b]—three readings (6) | | .44 | .48 | .45 | .45 | .47 | .48 | .46 |
| *Combinations* | | | | | | | | |
| 1,2 | .49 | | | | | | | |
| 1,3 | .52 | | | | | | | |
| 2,3 | .52 | | | | | | | |
| 1,4 | | .48 | .53 | .51 | .51 | .54 | .52 | .52 |
| 1,5 | | .49 | .54 | .52 | .52 | .55 | .54 | .53 |
| 1,6 | | .49 | .55 | .52 | .53 | .56 | .55 | .53 |
| 2,4 | | .46 | .51 | .48 | .48 | .52 | .50 | .49 |
| 2,5 | | .47 | .53 | .50 | .50 | .54 | .53 | .51 |
| 2,6 | | .48 | .54 | .50 | .51 | .55 | .55 | .52 |
| 3,4 | | .53 | .57 | .56 | .55 | .57 | .56 | .56 |
| 3,5 | | .53 | .58 | .56 | .56 | .58 | .57 | .56 |
| 3,6 | | .53 | .59 | .56 | .56 | .58 | .58 | .57 |
| 1,2,4 | | .50 | .54 | .52 | .52 | .55 | .53 | .53 |
| 1,3,4 | | .53 | .57 | .56 | .55 | .57 | .56 | .56 |
| 2,3,4 | | .53 | .57 | .56 | .55 | .57 | .56 | .56 |
| 1,2,5 | | .50 | .55 | .53 | .53 | .56 | .55 | .54 |
| 1,3,5 | | .53 | .58 | .56 | .56 | .58 | .57 | .56 |
| 2,3,5 | | .53 | .59 | .56 | .56 | .58 | .58 | .57 |
| 1,2,6 | | .50 | .56 | .53 | .53 | .57 | .57 | .54 |
| 1,3,6 | | .53 | .59 | .56 | .56 | .58 | .58 | .57 |
| 2,3,6 | | .53 | .59 | .56 | .56 | .58 | .59 | .57 |

a. See note a in Table F.13.
b. See note b in Table F.13.

*Table F.17. Multiple correlations between alternative predictor sets and freshman English course grade for Sample A (267 cases)*

| Predictor(s) | Essay used as predictor[a] | | | | | | | Average R |
|---|---|---|---|---|---|---|---|---|
| | None | N1 | N2 | E1 | E2 | P1 | P2 | |
| TSWE (1) | .41 | | | | | | | |
| SAT-V (2) | .44 | | | | | | | |
| ECT (3) | — | | | | | | | |
| Essay[b]—one reading (4) | | .37 | .37 | .32 | .37 | .46 | .43 | .39 |
| Essay[b]—two readings (5) | | .42 | .41 | .36 | .42 | .50 | .48 | .43 |
| Essay[b]—three readings (6) | | .44 | .44 | .38 | .44 | .52 | .50 | .45 |
| *Combinations* | | | | | | | | |
| 1,2 | .46 | | | | | | | |
| 1,4 | | .46 | .49 | .44 | .47 | .52 | .51 | .48 |
| 1,5 | | .47 | .49 | .45 | .49 | .54 | .54 | .50 |
| 1,6 | | .48 | .50 | .45 | .50 | .55 | .55 | .51 |
| 2,4 | | .49 | .50 | .47 | .50 | .55 | .54 | .51 |
| 2,5 | | .50 | .52 | .48 | .51 | .57 | .57 | .53 |
| 2,6 | | .51 | .53 | .48 | .52 | .58 | .58 | .53 |
| 1,2,4 | | .50 | .51 | .48 | .51 | .55 | .55 | .52 |
| 1,2,5 | | .51 | .52 | .49 | .52 | .57 | .57 | .53 |
| 1,2,6 | | .51 | .53 | .49 | .53 | .58 | .58 | .54 |

a. See note a in Table F.13.
b. See note b in Table F.13.

## Table F.18. Multiple correlations between alternative predictor sets and freshman English course grade for Sample B (210 cases)

| Predictor(s) | Essay used as predictor[a] | | | | | | | Average R |
|---|---|---|---|---|---|---|---|---|
| | None | N1 | N2 | E1 | E2 | P1 | P2 | |
| TSWE (1) | .45 | | | | | | | |
| SAT-V (2) | .48 | | | | | | | |
| ECT (3) | .45 | | | | | | | |
| Essay[b]—one reading (4) | | .40 | .39 | .37 | .43 | .48 | .41 | .41 |
| Essay[b]—two readings (5) | | .44 | .45 | .42 | .48 | .53 | .46 | .46 |
| Essay[b]—three readings (6) | | .46 | .47 | .43 | .50 | .55 | .48 | .48 |
| *Combinations* | | | | | | | | |
| 1,2 | .51 | | | | | | | |
| 1,3 | .47 | | | | | | | |
| 2,3 | .51 | | | | | | | |
| 1,4 | | .50 | .51 | .48 | .52 | .55 | .53 | .52 |
| 1,5 | | .51 | .53 | .50 | .54 | .57 | .55 | .53 |
| 1,6 | | .51 | .54 | .50 | .55 | .58 | .56 | .54 |
| 2,4 | | .53 | .55 | .52 | .55 | .59 | .56 | .55 |
| 2,5 | | .54 | .57 | .54 | .57 | .61 | .58 | .57 |
| 2,6 | | .55 | .58 | .54 | .58 | .62 | .59 | .58 |
| 3,4 | | .50 | .52 | .49 | .52 | .55 | .52 | .52 |
| 3,5 | | .51 | .54 | .51 | .55 | .57 | .55 | .54 |
| 3,6 | | .52 | .55 | .51 | .56 | .58 | .56 | .55 |
| 1,2,4 | | .54 | .56 | .53 | .56 | .59 | .57 | .56 |
| 1,3,4 | | .51 | .53 | .50 | .53 | .56 | .54 | .53 |
| 2,3,4 | | .54 | .56 | .54 | .56 | .59 | .57 | .56 |
| 1,2,5 | | .55 | .57 | .54 | .58 | .61 | .59 | .57 |
| 1,3,5 | | .52 | .55 | .51 | .55 | .58 | .56 | .55 |
| 2,3,5 | | .55 | .58 | .55 | .58 | .61 | .59 | .58 |
| 1,2,6 | | .55 | .58 | .55 | .59 | .62 | .59 | .58 |
| 1,3,6 | | .52 | .56 | .52 | .56 | .59 | .56 | .55 |
| 2,3,6 | | .55 | .59 | .55 | .59 | .62 | .59 | .58 |

a. See note a in Table F.13.
b. See note b in Table F.13.

## Table F.19. Multiple correlations between alternative predictor sets and freshman English course grade for Sample C (141 cases)

| Predictor(s) | Essay used as predictor[a] | | | | | | | Average R |
|---|---|---|---|---|---|---|---|---|
| | None | N1 | N2 | E1 | E2 | P1 | P2 | |
| TSWE (1) | .42 | | | | | | | |
| SAT-V (2) | .37 | | | | | | | |
| ECT (3) | .41 | | | | | | | |
| Essay[b]—one reading (4) | | .40 | .42 | .39 | .42 | .45 | .44 | .42 |
| Essay[b]—two readings (5) | | .45 | .48 | .43 | .47 | .50 | .50 | .47 |
| Essay[b]—three readings (6) | | .47 | .50 | .46 | .49 | .52 | .53 | .50 |
| *Combinations* | | | | | | | | |
| 1,2 | .44 | | | | | | | |
| 1,3 | .43 | | | | | | | |
| 2,3 | .42 | | | | | | | |
| 1,4 | | .47 | .51 | .48 | .49 | .53 | .52 | .50 |
| 1,5 | | .48 | .53 | .49 | .52 | .55 | .55 | .52 |
| 1,6 | | .49 | .54 | .50 | .53 | .56 | .57 | .53 |
| 2,4 | | .45 | .49 | .45 | .48 | .52 | .54 | .49 |
| 2,5 | | .47 | .52 | .48 | .51 | .55 | .55 | .51 |
| 2,6 | | .48 | .54 | .49 | .52 | .56 | .57 | .53 |
| 3,4 | | .47 | .50 | .47 | .49 | .52 | .54 | .50 |
| 3,5 | | .48 | .53 | .49 | .52 | .55 | .55 | .52 |
| 3,6 | | .49 | .55 | .50 | .53 | .56 | .56 | .53 |
| 1,2,4 | | .48 | .51 | .48 | .50 | .54 | .53 | .51 |
| 1,3,4 | | .48 | .51 | .48 | .50 | .53 | .52 | .50 |
| 2,3,4 | | .47 | .51 | .45 | .50 | .53 | .53 | .50 |
| 1,2,5 | | .49 | .54 | .50 | .52 | .56 | .56 | .53 |
| 1,3,5 | | .49 | .54 | .50 | .52 | .55 | .55 | .53 |
| 2,3,5 | | .51 | .54 | .50 | .52 | .56 | .55 | .53 |
| 1,2,6 | | .49 | .55 | .50 | .53 | .57 | .57 | .54 |
| 1,3,6 | | .49 | .55 | .50 | .53 | .56 | .57 | .53 |
| 2,3,6 | | .49 | .55 | .50 | .53 | .57 | .57 | .54 |

a. See note a in Table F.13.
b. See note b in Table F.13.

*Table F.20. Multiple correlations between alternative predictor sets and freshman English course grade for Sample D (94 cases)*

| Predictor(s) | Essay used as predictor[a] | | | | | | | Average R |
| | None | N1 | N2 | E1 | E2 | P1 | P2 | |
| --- | --- | --- | --- | --- | --- | --- | --- | --- |
| TSWE (1) | .45 | | | | | | | |
| SAT-V (2) | .42 | | | | | | | |
| ECT (3) | .44 | | | | | | | |
| Essay[b]—one reading (4) | | .42 | .46 | .47 | .42 | .43 | .37 | .43 |
| Essay[b]—two readings (5) | | .47 | .52 | .51 | .48 | .47 | .43 | .48 |
| Essay[b]—three readings (6) | | .49 | .55 | .53 | .50 | .49 | .47 | .51 |
| *Combinations* | | | | | | | | |
| 1,2 | .47 | | | | | | | |
| 1,3 | .46 | | | | | | | |
| 2,3 | .46 | | | | | | | |
| 1,4 | | .48 | .54 | .53 | .51 | .53 | .50 | .52 |
| 1,5 | | .50 | .56 | .55 | .53 | .54 | .52 | .53 |
| 1,6 | | .51 | .58 | .56 | .54 | .55 | .53 | .55 |
| 2,4 | | .48 | .54 | .52 | .50 | .53 | .50 | .51 |
| 2,5 | | .50 | .57 | .55 | .53 | .55 | .53 | .54 |
| 2,6 | | .51 | .58 | .56 | .54 | .56 | .54 | .55 |
| 3,4 | | .49 | .54 | .54 | .51 | .52 | .50 | .52 |
| 3,5 | | .51 | .57 | .56 | .54 | .54 | .52 | .54 |
| 3,6 | | .51 | .59 | .57 | .55 | .55 | .53 | .55 |
| 1,2,4 | | .50 | .55 | .54 | .53 | .55 | .52 | .53 |
| 1,3,4 | | .49 | .55 | .54 | .52 | .53 | .51 | .52 |
| 2,3,4 | | .50 | .55 | .54 | .52 | .54 | .52 | .53 |
| 1,2,5 | | .51 | .58 | .58 | .54 | .56 | .54 | .55 |
| 1,3,5 | | .51 | .57 | .56 | .54 | .55 | .53 | .54 |
| 2,3,5 | | .51 | .58 | .56 | .54 | .56 | .54 | .55 |
| 1,2,6 | | .52 | .59 | .57 | .55 | .57 | .55 | .56 |
| 1,3,6 | | .52 | .59 | .57 | .55 | .55 | .54 | .55 |
| 2,3,6 | | .52 | .59 | .57 | .55 | .56 | .55 | .56 |

a. See note a in Table F.13.
b. See note b in Table F.13.

Table F.21. Holistic reader score intercorrelations

| Essay/reader[a] | Mean | SD[b] | Variable number | | | | | | | | | | | | | | | | | |
|---|---|---|---|---|---|---|---|---|---|---|---|---|---|---|---|---|---|---|---|---|---|
| | | | 1 | 2 | 3 | 4 | 5 | 6 | 7 | 8 | 9 | 10 | 11 | 12 | 13 | 14 | 15 | 16 | 17 | 18 |
| 1. N1R1 | 3.65 | 1.06 | 1.00 | | | | | | | | | | | | | | | | | |
| 2. N1R2 | 3.79 | .93 | .58 | 1.00 | | | | | | | | | | | | | | | | |
| 3. N1R3 | 3.78 | 1.23 | .52 | .46 | 1.00 | | | | | | | | | | | | | | | |
| 4. N2R1 | 3.76 | 1.05 | .38 | .46 | .36 | 1.00 | | | | | | | | | | | | | | |
| 5. N2R2 | 3.81 | 1.13 | .44 | .56 | .47 | .57 | 1.00 | | | | | | | | | | | | | |
| 6. N2R3 | 3.80 | 1.33 | .24 | .23 | .32 | .51 | .48 | 1.00 | | | | | | | | | | | | |
| 7. E1R1 | 3.45 | 1.11 | .37 | .48 | .38 | .45 | .46 | .34 | 1.00 | | | | | | | | | | | |
| 8. E1R2 | 3.73 | .97 | .35 | .42 | .31 | .44 | .42 | .33 | .59 | 1.00 | | | | | | | | | | |
| 9. E1R3 | 3.72 | 1.12 | .33 | .40 | .39 | .50 | .48 | .44 | .64 | .62 | 1.00 | | | | | | | | | |
| 10. E2R1 | 3.53 | 1.08 | .29 | .46 | .34 | .35 | .37 | .30 | .43 | .36 | .39 | 1.00 | | | | | | | | |
| 11. E2R2 | 3.66 | 1.01 | .31 | .39 | .37 | .35 | .34 | .33 | .36 | .37 | .40 | .61 | 1.00 | | | | | | | |
| 12. E2R3 | 3.64 | 1.09 | .30 | .37 | .44 | .38 | .38 | .41 | .49 | .49 | .58 | .62 | .57 | 1.00 | | | | | | |
| 13. P1R1 | 3.98 | 1.18 | .30 | .42 | .32 | .27 | .42 | .26 | .34 | .34 | .31 | .43 | .35 | .36 | 1.00 | | | | | |
| 14. P1R2 | 3.74 | 1.29 | .30 | .42 | .34 | .27 | .35 | .24 | .38 | .38 | .30 | .42 | .43 | .42 | .68 | 1.00 | | | | |
| 15. P1R3 | 3.72 | 1.19 | .19 | .32 | .21 | .25 | .32 | .21 | .34 | .34 | .32 | .40 | .36 | .30 | .59 | .68 | 1.00 | | | |
| 16. P2R1 | 4.18 | 1.10 | .29 | .36 | .25 | .32 | .36 | .31 | .34 | .30 | .36 | .34 | .30 | .35 | .46 | .53 | .49 | 1.00 | | |
| 17. P2R2 | 4.01 | 1.21 | .22 | .36 | .23 | .27 | .29 | .21 | .34 | .27 | .32 | .40 | .35 | .39 | .49 | .56 | .48 | .68 | 1.00 | |
| 18. P2R3 | 3.78 | 1.26 | .23 | .29 | .16 | .29 | .37 | .24 | .23 | .29 | .29 | .30 | .31 | .28 | .41 | .44 | .45 | .56 | .55 | 1.00 |

a. N stands for narrative, E for expository, P for persuasive, R for reader.
b. Standard Deviation.

*Table F.22. Intercorrelations of reader error counts and error count reliability estimates*

| Variable/ error type/ reader number | Variable number 1 | 2 | 3 | 4 | 5 | 6 | 7 | 8 | 9 | 10 | 11 | 12 | 13 | 14 | 15 | 16 | 17 | 18 |
|---|---|---|---|---|---|---|---|---|---|---|---|---|---|---|---|---|---|---|
| 1. Grammar, R1 | 1.00 | | | | | | | | | | | | | | | | | |
| 2. Usage, R1 | .46 | 1.00 | | | | | | | | | | | | | | | | |
| 3. S. str., R1 | .45 | .49 | 1.00 | | | | | | | | | | | | | | | |
| 4. Punct., R1 | .12 | .30 | .22 | 1.00 | | | | | | | | | | | | | | |
| 5. Spelling, R1 | .22 | .43 | .46 | .26 | 1.00 | | | | | | | | | | | | | |
| 6. Cap., etc., R1 | .20 | .21 | .29 | .26 | .37 | 1.00 | | | | | | | | | | | | |
| 7. Grammar, R2 | .70^c | .50 | .42 | .26 | .30 | .21 | 1.00 | | | | | | | | | | | |
| 8. Usage, R2 | .68 | .71^c | .54 | .14 | .44 | .24 | .62 | 1.00 | | | | | | | | | | |
| 9. S. str., R2 | .48 | .59 | .68^c | .40 | .41 | .28 | .48 | .56 | 1.00 | | | | | | | | | |
| 10. Punct., R2 | .23 | .52 | .40 | .61^c | .48 | .36 | .49 | .41 | .52 | 1.00 | | | | | | | | |
| 11. Spelling, R2 | .15 | .41 | .42 | .17 | .93^c | .37 | .22 | .41 | .34 | .46 | 1.00 | | | | | | | |
| 12. Cap., ect., R2 | .37 | .34 | .48 | .34 | .34 | .58^c | .39 | .33 | .39 | .38 | .30 | 1.00 | | | | | | |
| 13. GUSS^a, R1 | .81^d | .85^d | .73^d | .27 | .44 | .28 | .68 | .81 | .71 | .48 | .39 | .47 | 1.00 | | | | | |
| 14. PSC^b, R1 | .23 | .45 | .45 | .75^d | .81^d | .69^d | .35 | .39 | .50 | .66 | .72 | .50 | .46 | 1.00 | | | | |
| 15. GUSS^a, R2 | .75 | .72 | .63 | .29 | .46 | .28 | .85^d | .90^d | .76^d | .55 | .39 | .43 | .88^c | .48 | 1.00 | | | |
| 16. PSC^b, R2 | .25 | .54 | .52 | .42 | .87 | .48 | .41 | .49 | .50 | .78^d | .90^d | .51^d | .53 | .83^c | .55 | 1.00 | | |
| 17. Total, R1 | .57^d | .73^d | .67^d | .63^d | .75^d | .59^d | .58 | .68 | .69 | .68 | .67 | .57 | .82^d | .89^d | .76 | .81 | 1.00 | |
| 18. Total, R2 | .55 | .70 | .65 | .41 | .77 | .44 | .69^d | .77^d | .70^d | .77^d | .75^d | .54^d | .78 | .76 | .86^d | .90^d | .90^c | 1.00 |

Error count reliability estimates

| | |
|---|---|
| Grammar | .82 |
| Usage | .83 |
| Sentence structure | .81 |
| Punctuation | .75 |
| Spelling | .96 |
| Capitalization, etc. | .73 |
| GUSS | .93 |
| PSC | .91 |
| Total | .95 |

*Note:* Correlations in excess of .24 are statistically significant at the .01 level; correlations in excess of .32 are statistically significant at the .001 level.

a. Grammar, usage, and sentence structure error total.

b. Punctuation, spelling, and capitalization, etc., total.

c. Underlined correlations are interrater correlations of counts of the same types of errors. Stepped up, they represent reliabilities for error count averages across readers.

d. Artificially inflated by part-whole confounding.

## Table F.23. Analysis of variance—all modes, Sample A (N=270)

| Source | Sum of squares | df | Mean square | F | Estimates of variance components |
|---|---|---|---|---|---|
| Mean | 68636.5630 | 1 | 68636.56296 | | 14.11874 |
| Subjects (S) | 2613.1037 | 269 | 9.71414 | | 0.47017 |
| Mode (M) | 62.2679 | 2 | 31.13395 | | 0.01204 |
| Topics (T) | 13.6827 | 3 | 4.56091 | | 0.00351 |
| Readers (R) | 45.2210 | 6 | 7.53683 | | 0.01177 |
| S × M | 997.7321 | 538 | 1.85452 | | 0.10058 |
| S × T | 919.9840 | 807 | 1.14000 | 2.34** | 0.21727 |
| S × R | 967.1123 | 1614 | 0.59920 | 1.23** | 0.05551 |
| T × R | 6.4062 | 6 | 1.06770 | 2.19* | 0.00215 |
| S × T × R (error) | 787.9272 | 1614 | 0.48818 | | 0.48818 |

\* p < .05
\*\* p < .01

## Table F.24. Analysis of variance—narrative mode, Sample A (N=270)

| Source | Sum of squares | df | Mean square | F | Estimates of variance components |
|---|---|---|---|---|---|
| Mean | 22931.40691 | 1 | 22931.49691 | | 14.15233 |
| Subjects (S) | 1084.66975 | 269 | 4.03223 | | 0.45816 |
| Topics (T) | 0.93889 | 1 | 0.93889 | | − 0.00014 |
| Readers (R) | 2.97901 | 2 | 1.48951 | | 0.00169 |
| S × T | 312.56111 | 269 | 1.16194 | 2.04* | 0.19767 |
| S × R | 371.35432 | 538 | 0.69025 | 1.21* | 0.06066 |
| T × R | 0.91481 | 2 | 0.45741 | 0.08 | − 0.00041 |
| S × T × R (error) | 306.08519 | 538 | 0.56893 | | 0.56893 |

\* p < .05

## Table F.25. *Analysis of variance—expository mode, Sample A (N=270)*

| Source | Sum of squares | df | Mean square | F | Estimates of variance components |
|---|---|---|---|---|---|
| Mean | 21197.28395 | 1 | 21197.28395 | | 13.07961 |
| Subjects (S) | 1066.04938 | 269 | 3.96301 | | 0.45372 |
| Topics (T) | 0.12099 | 1 | 0.12099 | | −0.00205 |
| Readers (R) | 13.08272 | 2 | 6.54136 | | 0.00985 |
| S × T | 291.87901 | 269 | 1.08505 | 2.94* | 0.23847 |
| S × R | 282.68395 | 538 | 0.52525 | 1.42* | 0.07781 |
| T × R | 2.13457 | 2 | 1.06728 | 2.89 | 0.00258 |
| S × T × R (error) | 198.86543 | 538 | 0.36964 | | 0.36964 |

* p < .01

## Table F.26. *Analysis of variance—persuasive mode, Sample A (N=270)*

| Source | Sum of squares | df | Mean square | F | Estimates of variance components |
|---|---|---|---|---|---|
| Mean | 24570.0500 | 1 | 24570.05000 | | 15.14835 |
| Subjects (S) | 1460.1167 | 269 | 5.42794 | | 0.69980 |
| Topics (T) | 12.6228 | 1 | 12.62284 | | 0.01271 |
| Readers (R) | 29.1593 | 2 | 14.57963 | | 0.02379 |
| S × T | 315.5438 | 269 | 1.17303 | 2.23** | 0.21568 |
| S × R | 313.1741 | 538 | 0.58211 | 1.11 | 0.02806 |
| T × R | 3.3568 | 2 | 1.67840 | 3.19* | 0.00427 |
| S × T × R (error) | 282.9765 | 538 | 0.52598 | | 0.52508 |

 * p < .05
** p < .01

## Table F.27. Analysis of variance—all modes, Sample D (N = 94)

| Source | Sum of squares | df | Mean square | F | Estimates of variance components |
|---|---|---|---|---|---|
| Mean | 26065.53251 | 1 | 26065.53251 | | 15.39901 |
| Subjects (S) | 872.41194 | 93 | 9.38077 | | 0.46539 |
| Modes (M) | 35.87707 | 2 | 17.93853 | | 0.02709 |
| Topics (T) | 0.92730 | 3 | 0.30910 | | −0.00098 |
| Readers (R) | 11.34043 | 6 | 1.89007 | | 0.00868 |
| S × M | 302.34515 | 186 | 1.62551 | | 0.10362 |
| S × T | 253.23936 | 279 | 0.90767 | 1.87** | 0.14105 |
| S × R | 323.99291 | 558 | 0.58063 | 1.20* | 0.04806 |
| T × R | 0.97163 | 6 | 0.16194 | 0.33 | −0.00343 |
| S × T × R (error) | 270.36170 | 558 | 0.48452 | | 0.48452 |

\* $p < .05$
\*\* $p < .01$

## Table F.28. Analysis of variance—narrative mode, Sample D (N = 94)

| Source | Sum of squares | df | Mean square | F | Estimates of variance components |
|---|---|---|---|---|---|
| Mean | 8418.512411 | 1 | 8418.512411 | | 14.91892 |
| Subjects (S) | 418.987589 | 93 | 4.505243 | | 0.54740 |
| Topics (T) | 0.143617 | 1 | 0.143617 | | −0.00162 |
| Readers (R) | 1.663121 | 2 | 0.831560 | | 0.00414 |
| S × T | 110.023050 | 93 | 1.183044 | 1.98* | 0.19488 |
| S × R | 118.336879 | 186 | 0.636220 | 1.06 | 0.01891 |
| T × R | 0.031915 | 2 | 0.015957 | 0.03 | −0.00620 |
| S × T × R (error) | 111.301418 | 186 | 0.598395 | | 0.59839 |

\* $p < .01$

## Table F.29. Analysis of variance—expository mode, Sample D (N=94)

| Source | Sum of squares | df | Mean square | F | Estimates of variance components |
|---|---|---|---|---|---|
| Mean | 8082.0 | 1 | 8082.0 | | 14.32426 |
| Subjects (S) | 374.54 | 93 | 4.0273 | | 0.50198 |
| Topics (T) | 0.00177 | 1 | 0.00177 | | −0.00210 |
| Readers (R) | 0.39716 | 2 | 0.19858 | | −0.00095 |
| S × T | 71.832 | 93 | 0.77238 | 2.46* | −0.15281 |
| S × R | 103.60 | 186 | 0.55700 | 1.77* | 0.12152 |
| T × R | 0.2695 | 2 | 0.13475 | 0.43 | −0.00191 |
| S × T × R (error) | 58.397 | 186 | 0.31396 | | 0.31396 |

* p < .01

## Table F.30. Analysis of variance—persuasive mode, Sample D (N=94)

| Source | Sum of squares | df | Mean square | F | Estimates of variance components |
|---|---|---|---|---|---|
| Mean | 9600.93794 | 1 | 9600.93794 | | 17.00803 |
| Subjects (S) | 381.22872 | 93 | 4.09923 | | 0.55403 |
| Topics (T) | 0.78191 | 1 | 0.78191 | | 0.00078 |
| Readers (R) | 9.28014 | 2 | 4.64007 | | 0.02286 |
| S × T | 71.38475 | 93 | 0.76758 | 1.42* | 0.07546 |
| S × R | 102.05319 | 186 | 0.54867 | 1.01 | 0.00374 |
| T × R | 0.67021 | 2 | 0.33511 | 0.62 | −0.00219 |
| S × T × R (error) | 100.66312 | 186 | 0.54120 | | 0.54120 |

* p < .05

# References

Anastasi, A. 1982. *Psychological testing*. 5th ed. New York: Macmillan.

Arbeiter, S. 1984. *Profiles: College-bound seniors, 1984*. New York: College Entrance Examination Board.

Braun, H. 1986. *Calibration of essay readers*. ETS Research Report no. 86-9. Princeton, New Jersey: Educational Testing Service.

Breland, H. M. 1983. *The direct assessment of writing skill: A measurement review*. College Board Report no. 83-6 (ETS Research Report no. 83-32). New York: College Entrance Examination Board.

Breland, H. M., and R. Duran. 1985. Assessing English composition skills in Spanish-speaking populations. *Educational and Psychological Measurement* 45:309–18.

Breland, H., and J. Gaynor. 1979. A comparison of direct and indirect assessments of writing skill. *Journal of Educational Measurement* 16:119–28.

Breland, H. M., and P. A. Griswold. 1982. Use of a performance test as a criterion in a differential validity study. *Journal of Educational Psychology* 74:713–21.

Breland, H. M., and R. J. Jones. 1984. *Perceptions of writing skills*. Princeton, New Jersey: Educational Testing Service.

Breland, H. M., D. A. Rock, J. Grandy, and J. W. Young. 1984. *Linear models of writing assessments*. ETS Research Memorandum (RM-84-2). Princeton, New Jersey: Educational Testing Service.

Britton, J., et al. 1975. *The development of writing abilities (11–18)*. London: Macmillan Education.

Camp, R. 1983. The ETS writing portfolio: A new kind of assessment. Paper delivered at the National Council for Measurement in Education.

Camp R. 1985. The writing folder in postsecondary assessment. In *Directions and misdirections in English evaluation*, ed. P. J. A. Evans. Ottawa, Canada: Council of Teachers of English. Distributed by Boynton/Cook, Upper Montclair, New Jersey.

Coffman, W. 1966. On the validity of essay tests of achievement. *Journal of Educational Measurement* 3:151–56.

Coffman, W. 1971. Essay examinations. In *Educational Measurement*, ed. R. L. Thorndike. 2d ed. Washington, D.C.: American Council on Education.

Cohen, J., and P. Cohen. 1975. *Applied multiple regression/correlation analysis for the behavioral sciences*. Hillsdale, New Jersey: Erlbaum.

Diederich, P. 1974. *Measuring growth in English*. Urbana, Illinois: National Council of Teachers of English.

Emig, J. 1971. *The composing processes of twelfth graders*. Urbana, Illinois: National Council of Teachers of English.

Faigley, L., and S. Witte. 1981. Analyzing revision. *College Composition and Communication* 32:400–14.

Field, J., and R. Weiss. 1984. *Cases for composition*. 2d ed. Boston: Little, Brown.

Flower, L., and J. R. Hayes. 1981. A cognitive process theory of writing. *College Composition and Communication* 32:365–87.

Follman, J., and J. Anderson. 1967. An investigation of the reliability of five procedures for grading English themes. *Research in Teaching of English* 1:190–200.

French, J. 1962. Schools of thought in judging excellence of English themes. Proceedings of the 1961 Invitational Conference on Testing Problems. Princeton, New Jersey: Educational Testing Service.

Godshalk, F., F. Swineford, and W. Coffman. 1966. *The measurement of writing ability*. Research Monograph no. 6. New York: College Entrance Examination Board.

Hopkins, T. 1921. The marking system of the College Entrance Examination Board. Harvard Monographs in Education, ser. 1, no. 2. Cambridge: Graduate School of Education, Harvard University.

Huddleston, E. 1954. Measurement of writing ability at the college-entrance level: Objective vs. subjective testing techniques. *Journal of Experimental Psychology* 22:165–213.

Hull, G. 1984. Assessing errors in writing. Paper presented at annual meeting of the American Educational Research Association, New Orleans.

Joreskog, K. G., and D. Sorbom, 1985. Lisrel 6, Analysis of linear structural relationships by the method of maximum likelihood: *User's Guide*. Mooresville, Indiana: Scientific Software, Inc.

Kinneavy, J. 1971. *A theory of discourse*. Englewood Cliffs, New Jersey: Prentice-Hall. Reprint. New York: Norton, 1980.

Markham, L. 1976. Influences of handwriting quality on teacher evaluation of written work. *American Educational Research Journal* 13: 227–83.

Moffett, J. 1968. *Teaching the universe of discourse*. Boston: Houghton Mifflin.

Moss, P., N. Cole, and C. Khampalikit. 1982. A comparison of procedures to assess written language skills at grades 4, 7, and 10. *Journal of Educational Measurement* 19 (1): 37–47.

Noyes, E. 1963. Essay and objective tests in English. *College Board Review* 49:7–10.

Perl, S. 1980. Understanding composing. *College Composition and Communication* 31:363–69.

Quellmalz, E., F. Capell, and C. Chou. 1982. Effects of discourse and response mode on the measurement of writing competence. *Journal of Educational Measurement* 19 (4): 241–58.

Ruth, L., and C. Keech. 1982. Designing prompts for holistic writing assessments: Knowledge from theory, research, and practice. In *Properties of writing tasks: A study for alternative procedures for holistic writing assessment*. Berkeley, California: Bay Area Writing Project, University of California. Eric Document Reproduction Service no. ED 230 576.

Ruth, L., and S. Murphy. 1984. Designing topics for writing assessment: Problems of meaning. *College Composition and Communication* 35:410–22.

Ruth, L., and S. Murphy. 1986. *Designing writing tasks for the assessment of writing*. Norwood, New Jersey: Ablex.

Sheppard, E. 1929. The effect of quality of penmanship on grades. *Journal of Educational Research* 19:102–5.

Sommers, N. 1980. Revision strategies of student writers and experienced adult writers. *College Composition and Communication* 31:378–88.

Stalnaker, J. 1936. The problem of the English examination. *Educational Record* 17 (suppl. 10).

Tedlock, D., and P. Jarvie. 1981. *Casebook rhetoric: A problem-solving approach to composition*. New York: Holt.

Traxler, A., and H. Anderson. 1935. Reliability of an essay test in English. *School Review* 43:534–40.

Werts, C., H. Breland, J. Grandy, and D. Rock. 1980. Using longitudinal data to estimate reliability in the presence of correlated measurement errors. *Educational and Psychological Measurement* 40:19–29.

White, E. 1985. *Teaching and assessing writing: Recent advances in understanding, evaluating, and improving student performance*. San Francisco: Jossey-Bass.

Witte, S., P. Meyer, R. Cherry, and M. Trachsel. (forthcoming.) *Holistic evaluation of writing: Issues in theory and practice*. New York: Guilford.